To Peace in Lebanon, the Middle East, and the World
to my mother & father, and the rest of the extended family.
to the past and to the future

To Dr. Alberto Gonzalez, for believing in the marginalized
in the times of crises.
To the Lebanese University, for educating the eager minds.
To Bowling Green State University for allowing voices.
To Nawal Hamd, a friend in the time of need.

TABLE OF CONTENTS

INTRODUCTION

"*Hezbollah*"[1] is a serious name. To the Americans it denotes the Lebanese extremists or the "terrorists" who killed the US marines in 1982. To a large audience of the Muslims, Hezbollah is a movement representing a marginalized group—the *Shia'a.* Also, to a large part of the Lebanese population, they are the guards of the border providing protection till the latest United Nations resolution 1701 in August 2006 which deployed the Lebanese army and the Unifel forces to the bordering South.

Having liberated South Lebanon in the year 2000 from the Israeli occupation, and leading a war against the Israeli army in July 2006, *Hezbollah* is a "hot and exotic" selection from the Arab platter, served at the American table of national security. A rhetorical analysis might save the meal from burning its inherent nutrition and the diner. But *Hezbollah*, or the *Party of God*, is a rhetorically complex matter. To many in the West population, just mentioning the group's Arabic name might raise many threats and insights from the people discussing it. In a highly tense political world, especially towards Arab-Muslims, disregarding such topic would be simply a matter of deliberate ignorance.

As Ghraib (2002) states, "*Hezbollah* is one of the largest and eminent sects in Lebanon, and maybe is the most known Islamic movement in the world. *Hezbollah*'s reputation turned bad when an alleged accusation that it was involved in the kidnapping of more than 80 Western hostages throughout the 1980s" (p. 9). I take a step forward to develop an argument that is rhetorical, intercultural, political, and religious and most importantly humane.

Chapter I
An Overview of the Islamic Resistance: the *Party of God*

Hezbollah, *the Culture*

In order to know something, researchers should at least invest in two positions, one of that by being an *etic*, outsider, and the other as an *emic*, insider (Lindlof 1995, p. 83). These two steps will add to the clarity and validity of the information gathering process as well as to the critical perspective. I experienced both positions. I have lived on a cultural borderline; one leg is in the American cultural pattern trying to figure out U.S. traditions that have been predominantly presented on the Arabic media networks in such television sitcoms "Seinfeld" and "Friends", and Arabic/ Westernized Lebanon. Another leg is situated in the realms of those traditions that I was raised on, practiced, and experienced in Lebanon within my predominant Islamic society.

The *Party of God* has been studied as a political agenda, rather than as a cultural performance. Scholars did not shift their attention to examine it in critical race studies or cultural performance ideology. Schbley (2000) discussed it in an article titled, "Torn between God, Family, and Money: The Changing Profile of Lebanon's Religious Terrorists". One of these changes is the use of the word *"terrorist"* as an identification of the group's political status. Hezbollah were distributing money (hard currency of US dollars) to the affected families after July's "open war" with Israel, which as well shows that it is not the need for money that is drawing people towards Jihad. It is rather an ideology, an advanced accumulation of progressive logic within the Islamic society in general and Hezbollah in particular. In the upcoming chapters, rhetoric will show that there is a complex process that comes into play in developing a martyr's figure. Simply, there is a need for a review of the movement's history and presence.

From a political perspective, the presence of *Hezbollah* helps to close a gap in the history of Lebanon, namely the borders gap [of North Israel/Palestine]. Also *Hezbollah* accounts for increased *Shia'a* representation in Lebanon after a long period of marginalization. Shia'a people of Lebanon were an additive to the Lebanese map after World War Two. Most historians admit the fact that they were only set in Lebanon not Syria because the Christians, Druze and Sunni people were convinced that they will need labor people. And thus most of the crafts men and women were among that sect until now.

However, all of these contributions are controversial. There is within that persistent movement, a natural transformation and shift from a narrow military objective to a broader social engagement. Schbley (2000) fixed *Hezbollah*'s identity by citing the terror attacks, "Hizbullah twice bombed U.S. embassy buildings" (p. 186). Meanwhile, in the year 2005, *Hezbollah* members were not bombing, but demonstrating (and demonstrating is a democratic right) in front of the American embassy in Lebanon. Delving into this project was an eye opening experience, and throughout the chapters I describe and critique the transformation. Conquergood (1983) explains that mechanism of transformation saying, "because cultures as well as people are continuously in a state of process, we might say a process of performance, there are special reflexive mechanisms in every culture for mirroring and monitoring behavior, for making action meaningful to the actors as well as the onlookers" (p. 29). This presentation is an element in the reflexive moment of *Hezbollah*.

Missing my culture began a journey of self-awareness; to know the self is an important step in knowing or studying the surrounding society. Because, after all the self is the knower, it is the instrument set for measurement in the following study. For instance, *Hezbollah* plays a filtering role in the society, a filter to Arab, Islam, and Shia'a. However, through the study, I play a role in being *Hezbollah's* filter.

Although I do not claim to fully understand my identity or my culture, because the deeper I went the more complex my surrounding became, yet Conquergood further explains this impression saying that "cultural performances make social life meaningful; they enable actors to interpret themselves to themselves as well to others, to become at once actor and audience" (p. 34). Hence, the least outcome would be that of an attempt to interpret. There is a thin line between narcissism and self-awareness where the latter can "open up a lively reflexivity which engenders growth, debate, and discovery" (Conquergood 1983, p. 34).

Experience Makes Perfect!

Born in the late seventies in Beirut, Lebanon, mine was labeled as the "war generation". However, my first awareness of the bitter meaning of war was in the year 1982, the Israeli invasion of Beirut. As a war generation, at five years old, I have experienced what it is like to hide in shelters, how a day, an hour, and a minute can make a difference in whether you stay alive or depart for good. War as well has developed and matured my senses. As a civilian, I was able to recognize whether it is time to hide, or whether it is safe to stay playing outside for a while.

My senses as well were able to recognize whether a bomb had passed, missed our house, or whether it was time to go down to the dark, damp and cold shelter. My senses matured to the extent that I could feel the timing of the battle, for I would hear the tanks move their positions in the mountains facing our house. Later on, I was able to anticipate a battle by calendar events. At other times, a suicide attack would result in a counter-bombing, hence expectation, hiding, and then relief— to some people it could be eternal relief—and to others this event would be only a minor interruption.

In brief, war, until the year 1990, has shaped how I look at the world, and what I want out of life. The best sentence that would summarize such an experience is that you can never appreciate peace unless you experience the dark side of war. A peace "without" is just like ethnicity, race, gender, class, and family relationships felt from "within and without", from the self and the surrounding community. The American civilians would empathize with such experience after the September 11th of the year 2001 tragedy and the insecurity they felt afterwards inside and outside the USA borders. And I am sure that the Lebanese people would share my state of affairs, for war never escapes social gatherings and reminiscing chats.

Abdullah, *the "Worshipper of God"*

Throughout the research, a recurring theme of the word *Abdullah* will be stated. *Abdullah*[2] overlaps the whole dissertation. Maybe because most of the wars we have witnessed have been wars of worship, wars over sacred places, over holy lands [or oil lands], over belief, wars over God: the Jewish, Christian, Muslim, Buddhists, etc. *Abdullah* also was the name of my cousin. He is a martyr. He is the first theme, in that ideological sense of presentation. *Abdullah*—meaning the worshipper of God—out of all the surrounding tragedies has awakened my senses to death (later on developed to be martyrdom). His father, a very well known doctor in Geology, died in a car accident leaving him, his two sisters and my aunt alone in this world to figure out its construction. *Abdullah* was very smart, reading his father's research at a very young age; he was recognized not only by the family, but as well by his country. Unfortunately, these hidden details as a young genius surfaced after his death—the case of many other great thinkers.

After the invasion of Beirut, Israel withdrew to South Lebanon, occupying part of it. One of the bordering cities in the South was my hometown *"Nabatieh"*. The derivative of the *"Anbat"* people who were traced to come from Jordan, and had a hand in building what is known as the *"Patra"* ruins. *"Nabat"* in the Arabic language was a name given to the first type of soil and water mixture that comes out of a water spring. This further explains why most people in the town were associated with construction. *Abdullah's* mission for what developed later on to be the *Party of God* was to disconnect

13

landmines planted by the Israeli armed forces in the mountains to keep away any *"Resistance fighters"* namely Lebanese and Palestinians. The narrative as told by my aunt (*Abdullah's* mother), who was not aware of his job, was that he told her that he is going to study with a friend. And then he was late coming back home. My aunt was worried, called my father, who went looking for him. Later on, one of his friends came to my aunt's home carrying the bad news that *Abdullah* died while he was putting off a landmine in the mountain. Going out in one piece, *Abdullah* was returned home in many pieces. My father's proverb during that era of the Lebanese war was strictly demonstrated "I did not die, but I have seen people who did".

More than fifteen years have passed. *Abdullah's* picture, in the main street of *Nabatieh*, stands next to many young photos of martyrs who died for liberating Lebanon. Taking the strategy of continuous commemoration through martyr's photos spread through out the liberated areas, like trees and flowers on the side walks, and road intersections, people still remember *Abdullah* although the colors of his picture have faded from the continuous exposure to the sun and other environmental factors making it more phantom-like, he is remembered too whenever conversations or speeches are made about nationalism, sacrifice and early genius, but he is remembered most by another *Abdullah* who looks exactly like him, and is fourteen years old now. *Abdullah*-the-second, *Abdullah* junior, or the second worshipper of God, is the nephew of *Abdullah*-the-first. And as many "South" Lebanese civilians put it, is the clear evidence set in the face of occupiers that they can take away our peace, our land, and the life of our children, but they cannot take away our soul and resistance. South Lebanon was liberated in the year 2000. *Abdullah* junior was one of the children who planted not a land mine, but the Lebanese flag on the same mountain where his uncle died. He is now enjoying partially the freedom, peace, and nationalism his uncle died for. Was it worth it? The answer will be in the coming chapters.

Lebanon, Modernity, and "Total War"

Lebanon, in particular, is a "site" of a modern dimension. Giddens (1991) explains that "modernity ushers is an era of 'total war' "(p. 15), which refers to Europe and the globe after World War II. One of the primary products of modernity is "certain distinct social forms, in which the most prominent is the nation-state" (Giddens 1991, p. 15). This is being strictly implemented after the "open war" between Israel and Hezbollah that took place on July 12th of 2006. Hezbollah has showed an attachment to the nation-state like no other time in its presence history, especially when the General Secretary announces that he will hand in the negotiation of the seized soldiers to the Head of the Lebanese Parliament Nabieh Berry. Other stands show clearly such recognition of the nation-state, especially when the plan for reconstruction where all the chaos that used to fill areas occupied by Shia'a are set towards more comprehensive-modern- organized-constructions and a dedication towards all inclusive participation in the government. Modern states, Giddens adds, "follow coordinated policies and plans on a geopolitical scale. As such, they are prime example of a more general feature of modernity, the rise of organization" (p. 16). This ideal of the autonomous nation-state figures largely in Lebanese social and political thought.

Further, Giddens summarizes the context by saying "the modern world is a runaway world: not only is the pace of social change much faster than in any prior system, so also is its scope, and the profoundness with which it affects pre-existing social practices and modes of behaviors" (p. 16). Investigating deeper, would uncover the presence of the *Party of God* as an ordering mechanism social, political, and economical norms in the Lebanese system reshaping and restoring in the Lebanese social world. Its legitimacy comes from a national recognition (partially to release the internal guilt of sacrifices, and changes brought by the organization), awaiting that of an international one, especially after the integration of *Hezbollah* in the political world of the Lebanese ministry. Hezbollah has been trying to gain the political acceptance through its delicate polices. Its strategies are to abide by UN resolutions, government integration and targeted relationships with some Western countries.

Research Questions

The *Party of God* has an indigenous nature. It is multilayered and multi dimensional. Sometimes, through out the study I will be using the word *Hezbollah*, in Arabic and other times I will be using the word *Party of God,* the English translation of *Hezbollah*, just to vary in tune, and meaning according to the test at play. A comprehensive study would only embark on such a topic through the usage of categorized representations of the movement's history and presence. In order to reveal the constitution of *Hezbollah* organization procedures, I have set some research questions to guide the study:

1. What is the rhetorical origin of the *Party of God*? What discourse created the *Party of God*? Out of what discursive context did the *Party of God* arise?

2. How does the *Party of God* mediate and accommodate diverse constructions of ethnicity, race and color through its

organizational structure? What are its manifestations within the Islamic religion?

3. How is leadership symbolically constructed within the *Party of God* organization?

4. What is the organizational reality of the *Party of God* as revealed by language codes and practices? How does language usage reinforce or contradict organizational goals?

Answering these questions would completely draft a curvilinear representation of *Hezbollah*. It would gradually lead to an interpretation and analysis of the party. Such comprehensive reporting also represent a look at the Arabic, Muslim rhetorical representations.

Rationale for the Rhetorical Study of Hezbollah

Various reasons contribute to the significance of *Hezbollah's* study: *Hezbollah* is a poorly understood movement. It is portrayed as a one-dimensional terrorist group. *Hezbollah* members are portrayed as plane hijackers, kidnappers and suicide bombers. But *Hezbollah* has a rhetorical life, even the rhetorical construction of the martyr is worth examination from a cultural perspective. *Hezbollah* employs and reflects a mix of rhetorical extensions, including that of it acting as a filter of Islamic rhetorical meanings. Such rhetorical extensions include photos, books, various types of publications, media broadcasting, and DVDs, etc. These influences and their projections are examined in key rhetorical moments, for example, the *"Liberation Wedding"* video-CD, that was broadcasted and released in the year 2000 after the liberation of South Lebanon this video-CD records and presents the lively, uninterrupted (no voice over) celebration throughout Lebanon.

The study will critique the rhetorical strategies employed by *Hezbollah* and interpret the construction of its various audiences, recruits, the Arab World, Lebanon, and the West. Through the study, the reader will encounter an exploration of how language constructs the movement's identity and purpose. *Hezbollah* faces a critical rhetorical challenge in its third decade. However, there are cures and remedies that are employed. Under such circumstances, an examination of the employed techniques would help bring forth an argument of (new) symbolic constructions within the group, especially after the "open war" with Israel that recently took place.

Various other reasons help in the development of a solid rationale behind the study of the *Party of God*, that of the Arabic-Islamic rhetoric: the study will provide an overview of the Arabic-Islamic rhetoric at play now. To the Western culture, such rhetoric has been ignored, deleted, translated, sketched, or/ and simply hidden from the world literature. Within such processes, Arabic rhetoric lost many essential messages that would greatly help in the advancement of literature, and literary criticism. This study will make an attempt to elucidate such rhetoric especially when considering *Hezbollah* as a type of filter that some, most, or even selected messages would pass through, hence renovating, rebuilding and recreating the old, as well as emphasizing its continuity.

An additional element of the rationale is the suggestion of a cultural bridge between the Middle East and the West. Societies nowadays are similar in condition to an Arabic proverb that describes them as "standing on a demon's palm". This means that any intense misunderstanding will be the small match that breaks the donkey's back. This match is not only capable of breaking backs, but also of lighting up a nuclear, or any type of war. Cultural bridges and cultural understanding are vitally in demand. This study will at least construct a bridge of understanding; for again an Arabic proverb says that "human are the enemies of what they don't know". Maybe once known, the match would neither break the donkey's back, nor light up war's fire, but the way towards cultural dialogue and understanding. Political, economical, and organizational exchange: the politics of peace, cultural inferences, and on top of it all the contribution(s) the study could add to the change process (re)occurring in the Middle East. Communication here serves best, in allowing a political conversation and pondering upon the components of such area. People and culture are in a state of process. Last but not least, culture, or organization is ever changing, it is not a constant phenomena, and it changes us and is changed by us. The Middle East as mentioned earlier is a dimension of cultural progresses and digresses. The study will allow the audience to identify such changes maybe to assimilate, or go with the flow, attribute, form rules, etc. No matter what the product might be, in one way or another such study is serving knowledge per-se.

Culture and Communication

In his article "The ideograph: A link between rhetoric and ideology", McGee (1980), states that "Human beings are conditioned, not directly to belief and behavior, but to a vocabulary of concepts that function as guides, warrants, reasons, or excuses for behavior and belief" (p. 445). Streeck (2002) indicates that culture is equivalent to civilization, "it denotes all the stuff that distinguishes human from other species" (p. 300). However, the question here is; what is the boundary of a culture? Where does it intersect with others and where does it diverge? How does culture develop to significant rituals and behavior patterns? Streeck answers "this stuff is unbound, does not come in discrete units, and is therefore not countable; it bears more resemblance to the weather than to a piece of land" (p. 301). The author adds, "We don't know where it comes from, how far it reaches and where it will go" (p. 301). Culture is not weather although it resembles its phenomena. Culture and weather because both depend on meaning and interpretation are ever changing. Culture is analogous to a piece of land indeed, for proximity reasons, the land that holds shared beliefs-a condensed piece of land with voices and materiality that is subject to continuous, harmonious-sometimes-change. Yet, we all know that land is, and has always been the material repository of cultures, an example would be that of the pharaoh graves, stone carvings, etc. These symbols and practices become the "vocabulary" for understanding heritage and social relations. Yet if culture were only a piece of land it would be a grave-like, within that piece of land there are factors that come into play, advancing it and keeping it alive.

There have been many perspectives for studying intercultural communication. Before I delve into such conceptualizations, I would like to point out to the inter/outer connectedness among culture, communication, and intercultural communication. The three might seem interrelated; however, they are not linear in their relation. There is a process that allows an exchange and allows them to feed into each other, similar to any system. For it is agreed among many scholars and writers such as Kroeber and Kluckhohn as cited by Kim and Gudykunst (1988) that culture consists of patterns, explicit and implicit, of and for behavior acquired and transmitted by symbols these are all constituting the distinctive achievements of human groups, I would add animals too. Culture as intercultural behavior and communication are not constant, it variability moves between space and time. Meaning sometimes place and historical or present presentations and experiences, and such variability varies as well with and among the human interactions.

Planalp (1999) approaches the culture issue from a different perspective. The author discusses the communication of emotion. Planalp says that "instead of a boxcar, we might appeal to the metaphor for communication that was introduced earlier—weaving a fabric together". She argues that communication is fabric with various colors woven together, "communication with one another is like weaving the fabric of social life together, using a wide range and varying amounts of color" (p. 41). Planalp adds "fabrics can range from extremely simple to very intricate designs"(p. 41). Similarly culture, it is a wide range from extremely simple to very intricate designs. Geertz (1973) observes a similar approach. He argues that in order to understand culture, one must see it from the members' point of view. In order to do this, Geertz believes researchers should become ethnographers. Interestingly, Geertz believes that any cultural analysis is incomplete because the deeper one goes the more complex the culture becomes. However it is important to note that although context, culture and co-culture are important aspects affecting communication, individuals are affected somewhat differently and other issues like class and socioeconomic status also play an important role.

Moreover, Planalp (1999) sums up that "clearly, some people have more talent and better developed communicative skills than others, but all draw on the resources of their culture, and other resources too numerous to mention" (p. 42). Drawing on personal experience, lived history, and observation, and focusing on rhetorical criticism and numerous resources such as analytical ability, I plan to bring an overview and critique of the *Party of God*. Yet, before I proceed into further investigations, I am going to sum up with a definition of culture relevant to the study and was used by Gaines (1994) which indicates that the term culture refers to "the way of life (that a group) hold(s) in common", and I use the term ethnic group to refer to "an identifiable set of individuals who socially interact and who maintain themselves over time...[and who are bound together by] some social structure and some system of norms governing [their] conduct" (p. 51).

The notion of performing culture is both a paradigmatic description of a phenomena as well as a theoretical position. Alexander (1999) states: "the practice of performing culture is an all encompassing aspect of our daily being, inclusive of rituals, customs, policies, and procedures" (p. 307). Inquiry is a process of creating and recreating knowledge in a three dimensional visions of the past, present, and future each in a varying stance. This essay takes as its primary object the cultural performance of the *Party of God*, from the previously mentioned dimensions, using autobiography (which might be considered the observed rhetorical dimension), and rhetoric as critical praxis. It seeks to address how the "Islamic Resistance" performs and negotiates culture in Lebanon, by bringing their articulated experiences, beliefs and strategies to bear upon the project. I then present an analysis of the formation of the culture, and a critical perspective of the present towards a more constructive future.

Scholars make commitments to particular ways of knowing, adopting different ways that efficiently and accurately serve the study. Moreover, experience enriches inquiry. Experience can be taken as well from three different dimensions, the biological, and the cultural and geographical (spatial) location.

This, experience can forecast a fourth dimension that of autobiography. Since all of these three characters of experience are members of the past dimension, yet existing in the present and continuous through the future, I would like to disregard the primary mode of linearity. From a biological perspective, carried in the blood, experience can be racial, such as genes, and defined in skin color such as an experience of being black, or brown or white. However, experience can as well be social, carrying indigenous cultural and religious beliefs, and affiliations with theological systems—Jewish, Christian, Muslim. Moreover, experience is spatial or geographical, such as the experience of living on the borders or intersection of cities, countries, or continents. An individual can express a dynamic experience of being a citizen of at least two countries, which is very common nowadays. "Belonging" is shaped by proximity, or ideology, etc. Hence, identity as conceptualized by postmodern scholars is indeed in flux and fragmented (Brown, 1995; Dickens and Fontana, 1994). Stability is momentary and contextual. Linearity and directness can only by achieved on paper; however, in practice it is curvilinear. For instance, to get from point A to B, any architect would draw a straight line on the paper, meanwhile, to get from point A to B in practice; all cultural architects would draw a curve. Thus, this argument would significantly explain the existing clash between linear versus spiral styles of communication, and would as well support postmodern scholars claim of the flux and fragmented identity.

Critical Method

The editor Burgchrdt (1995) presents Wichelns article "The literary criticism of oratory" (1925) by a statement saying:

"Embedded in biographies and histories of Literature, we find another type of criticism, that which combines the sketch of the mind and character with same discussion of style" (p. 5). While Wichelns thought of the solitary orator, this sentiment applies also to the organization, or movement. Its "mind and character" bear examination.

No matter how, where and when, and regardless of why, "we live our lives enveloped in symbols" (Foss 1989, p. 3). Rhetoric in its ultimate positive meaning means "the use of symbols to influence thought and action" (Foss 1989, p.4). Rhetoric the old version of the word communication suggests that it serves as a persuasive mechanism. Thus Foss explains; "rhetoric includes non discursive or non verbal symbols as well as discursive or verbal ones. Speeches, essays, conversations, poetry, novels, stories, television programs, films, art, architecture, plays, music, dance, advertisements, furniture, public demonstrations, and dress are all forms of rhetoric" (p. 4). *Hezbollah* employs a variety of rhetorical forms.

In using identification as his key term, Burke notes, "Traditionally, the key term for rhetoric is not identification, but persuasion" (p. 218).

In their presentation of the expansion of Western rhetoric, Golden, Berquist, and Coleman (1992) state that as a philosopher and metaphysician, Burke is impelled to give a philosophic treatment to the concept of unity or identity by an analysis of the nature of substance in general" (p. 219). Departing from the traditional focus on persuasion, Burke named common identity and shared meaning as the goal of rhetorical action.

Garret & Xiao (1994) explain;

"Thus, a discourse tradition directly or indirectly participates in a rhetorical situation in at least three ways: it generates needs and promotes interests in an audience that must to be met by new discourses; it cultivates an audience's expectations about the appropriate forms of discourses, the proper subject matter, the right modes of argumentation, and so forth in relation to a given circumstance; and also affects an audience's recognition and interpretation of a rhetorical exigency. It might not be going too far to say that, by creating or regenerating needs and promoting interests in an audience, a discourse tradition produces the conditions for its own continuity, recirculation, and reproduction" (p. 39).

Golden, Berquist, &Coleman, (1992) state, "To sum up, we are forced to distinguish between three kinds of speech: (1) the external, rhetorical speech, in the common meaning of the expression. (2) The speech that arises exclusively from a rationale proceeding. (3) The true rhetorical speech. This springs from the archai, non-deducible, moving and indicative, due to its original images (p. 314- 315). Rhetoric is closely related to postmodernism. Simply because rhetoric implies variability, non-fixedness, or better said the truth lies here in the eyes of the beholder.

Postmodernists exclaim similarly, when they claim as, mentioned previously, that truth is fragmented. Foss on the other hand proclaims, "The notion that reality is created through rhetoric means that reality is not fixed" (p. 4). Grassi (2001) articulates that rhetoric is not a techne, he pertains that "rhetoric is understood as ingenium, as the language-based human capacity to surpass what lies before us in our sensory awareness by catching sight of relationships, or similitudines among things (p. xv).

Rhetorically, it is only through languages that thought could directly or subvertly reveal itself. Grassi (2001) says "it is in language that the nature of man reveals itself, so that the teaching of language may have a purpose and a sense of its own, as well as acquiring philosophical significance" (p. 36). One can never underestimate the value of language. Simply put, "rhetorical criticism is the investigation and evaluation of rhetorical acts and artifacts for the purpose of understanding rhetorical processes" (Foss 1989, p. 5). There are purposes behind the presence of such science: building a better understanding of the world around us, and contributing to rhetorical theory. There are as well various formulations of the critical rhetorical method; on top of it is finding an artifact to study the *Party of God* a question to ask-its rhetorical origin- and a method for analyzing the artifact-the metaphoric method. Foss indicates; "if the metaphoric approach has been selected, the critic now would identify the metaphors in the artifact" (p. 19).

Foss indicates that the first extended treatment of metaphor was provided by Aristotle in *Rhetoric and Poetics*. Metaphor, he asserted, is the transference of a name from the object to which it has a natural application. This definition and other illustrations where enough to set the definition to our present time. Metaphor is not simply a decoration or an ornament that decorates our language "metaphor is a basic way by which the process of using symbols to know reality occurs" (Foss 1989, p. 188). Hence metaphoric descriptions transformed from being a narrow version of reality to an ultimate, more significant of and to it. As some scholars argue, all thought is metaphoric by origin and application. All thought has a screen which describes it. Therefore, "the purpose of metaphoric reality is to identify the major metaphors used by a rhetor(s) and to analyze how they create a particular reality" (Foss 1989, p. 191). The author of rhetorical criticism proceeds explaining the steps used in such process. These steps could be summed by examination, isolation, sorting, analysis, and assessment: (1) Examination of the artifact for a general sense of its dimensions and context, (2) Isolation of the metaphors in the artifact, (3) sorting of the metaphors into groups according to vehicle if the metaphors deal with the same tenor or subject or according to topic if the metaphors deal with various subjects; (4) analysis of the metaphors to discover how they function for the rhetor and audience, and (5) assessment of the metaphors used (Foss 1989, p. 191).

On the other hand, we should not disregard the fact that we (researchers, and public) most of the time are narrators. Foss describes such tendency as "recognition of our love of stories and our tendencies to reveal our perspectives on the world to others through stories have led to the study of narrative by scholars from wide range of disciplines" (p. 229). But what is narrative? A narrative is "a way of ordering and presenting a view of the world through a description of a situation involving characters, actions, and a settings that changes overtime" (p. 229).

There are various functions in which a narrative serves. Above all it helps us identify the central action of an experience; they help us decide what a particular experience is about. "From the infinite number of stimuli or data available to us, narratives help us sort through acts, characters, and situations so that a dominant central action point emerges" (p. 229). Thus, narratives have a particular service although bounded by an emergent context, that is dominated and dominates the act, the story. Narratives, as well has a particular procedure such as an analysis of the substance of the narrative, an analysis of the form, and an evaluation (Foss 989, p. 230).

Hezbollah *and Cultural Rhetoric*

Islam passed through many stages since its formation that led to a reformation, and the development of sects. As many religions and cultures, as they grow and expand, it is inevitable to prevent the formation of divisions. Along the way there forms historical aspects of battles, expansion, philosophizing the religion, etc. Yet, my concern here is with *Hezbollah* the *Party of God* or "Islamic Resistance" in particular. However, through such discussion, I will relate other developments in Islam in matters that concern the subject matter.

There are three basic reasons behind the formation of the Islamic Resistance or what is known as *Hezbollah*, these are: Israeli occupation of South Lebanon, international political pressure that was facing Lebanon at that time, and Muslim *Shai'a* weakness (marginalization) especially in South Lebanon at that time (Kassem 2002, p.7). Islam so far, is divided into two main sects, the Sunnis and the Shia'a groups. The Sunni believe that *"Alsahaba"* meaning the "wise ancestors" should rule the Islamic nation after Prophet Mohammad's death. While Shia'a group believe that Ali, Prophet Mohammad's cousin should rule the Islamic nation and they as well claim that Mohammad has claimed him as his ancestors in many speeches before his death. Ali was murdered by being stabbed in the back in the mosque. Such controversy has lead to the separation of the two sects as well to various battles; the major one was in Iraq and was called *"Karballa"* after the name of the city where it occurred where Mohammad's ancestors were killed (also called people of the house of the prophet), through a bloody battle. Since then, Muslims have been divided to what we may claim here as to the followers of the "wise ancestors" or the "relative ancestors".

Kassem (2002) explains that plenty of suspicions and

speculations surrounded the formation of the Islamic resistance group. However the sect started working in the public sphere, not in secret, the leaders started to announce its goals and ambitions. Due to the military occupation of South Lebanon, as a start the Islamic resistance group concentrated its efforts on working in the battlefield, as resistance to the Israeli occupation of South Lebanon. This did not give the sect time to fully announce their ideology and beliefs. However later on during and after the liberation of South Lebanon was taking place scholars and educated individuals started writing about the ideology of the sect, they gathered speeches of the leaders, they observed incidents of resistance, and tried to fit it within the macro and micro levels, the former is that of the social movement going in the Middle East, Arab world and the latter is the one taking place in Lebanon (p. 8).

However, such trials were moderate and humble; they did not express the complete ideology (social, political and economic) strategies of the Islamic Resistance in Lebanon. According to theology, the first strategy was the belief in Islam (p. 9). Islamic Resistance group practical strategy was strongly connected to Islam. To sum up the context surrounding the establishment of the Islamic Resistance, Kassem (2002) states:

The Islamic Resistance started in a very small group. People spread the word in villages, and avenues, then it would get wider, and started spreading to mosques, Friday prayer gatherings, and cultural ceremonies, such as Ashoura [the annual ceremony were Hussain, the nephew of Mohammad the prophet, and the people of the house, meaning Muhammad's kinship died in Krballaa, Iraq, to prove that they are the successors to rule the Muslim nation]. Kassem (2005) states, that mostly *Hezbollah* was the product of "an active clerical movement" (p. 13). The sized and limited formation was not an

29

impediment to the likely extended popularity that was later on proved through various incidents to be discussed in the following chapters especially when they were able to create a social movement within the entire Arab world through the "open war" with Israel. Such war increased their Arab popularity, world awareness and self esteem as an organization. However, this movement as Kassem indicates was humble as in its formation:

> "Initiated by a number of Islamic clerics just back from the holy schools of religion in Najaf in Iraq, the clerical teachings, speeches and cultural dialogue that ensued prompted many concerns and queries about Islam's proposed role in life. Until then, neither the cultural nor political scene-both preoccupied with various core concerns-had lent any attention to the Islamic direction or foreseen a role for it" (p. 14).

Activity was initially limited to leading the faithful at mosque prayers and teaching religion at village schools and nearby environs. Gradually, cultural events proliferated across various Lebanese districts, albeit within tight and limited circles. A number of young men with serious interest in Islam attended, and then so did the whole congregations. They all soon followed the clerics, forming small groups of individuals to watch over communities and playing educational and community service roles, always hinging on the cleric who oversaw and supported all efforts" (p. 13).

Kassem explains the role of leaders in spreading the word: Mussa Alsader studied in Iran (one of the most accredited school of Islam), and he started spreading the word in Tyer (a major city in South Lebanon), then he formed institutions for charity and orphans. He was a very charismatic man, with a strong personality and he was able to have many followers. He formed the High Islamic Shia'a Council which is an organization that takes care of the Muslim Shia'a errands and other organizations for healthcare, orphans, and various social benefits (p. 16). He was kidnapped in Libya after an invitation he received from the president Alkazafi, in the year 1987. Since then his destiny is unknown.

Mohammad Hassan Fadelallah formed Islamic organizations in Beirut that dealt with education religion, and social life of Muslims. He was in a close relationship with the Islamic Resistance in Lebanon. He was considered the first consultant in religious issues. This is due to his affiliation with Iranian (past) president *Alkhoumaini*. During his rule, *Alkhoumaini* was able to succeed in his overthrow in Iran and to transform the country into a Muslim State (Kassem 2002, p. 20).

These were regional reasons that led to the formation of *Hezbollah* in Lebanon. Kassem sums up the grounds which supports the Islamic Resistance and which are based on Islam and the *Qur'an*: Islam is the last message sent from God: (this is found in the proceeding holy books, the books of Abraham and Mosses). It is the complete religion for all human life. The world is set in precise order, God did not create humans out of anarchy, but to worship, and every human being has a job to accomplish through their life. Islam sets it in order. In addition, Kassem states that God has sent prophets such as Noah, Abraham, Mosses, Jesus, and Mohammed to bring the message of God: The first belief has to be in God (Allah):

> For we assuredly sent amongst every people an apostle, (with the command), serve God and eschew evil. Of the people were some whom God guided, and some on whom error became inevitably (established). So travel through the earth, and see what was the end of those who denied the truth" (*The Quran*, Sura XVI:Nahl).

31

The proceeding (sura) verse refers that God has already set the word, to believe in it. The best way that could reveal the presence of God is to look around and contemplate or travel, and then a person who denies the presence of God would see the end of those who disbelieved. In the following I am going to discuss some of the implications of the *The Quran*. There are many significations behind the naming, and it is not arbitrary in setting and formation. However these implications are going to be discussed gradually as I indicate the mission of *Hezbollah*. These were observations I developed along the discussions of the verses. The implications will help bring out the rational behind the Islamic belief, and make the ideas clear to the Western mentalities and society.

The first question that would be questionable is that God almighty is referencing a small insect [bee] through naming a whole verse after it! Bees are digital and timely insects [insects], meaning they form an organizational structure in communication and construction. Along the verses of the *Quran* there has been many references to bees, along them was the similitude between the heavenly houses (God promised) and the bees' comb. Such similitude might be an ironic example of a micro/macro level of resemblance. Those who believe-the *Quran* states-will have houses like the bees comb under which dwells rivers. A bee is timely and digital in which it follows the natural process in communication. In other words, when a bee wants to show its friends to the source of food; it dances in semi circles, forming shapes similar to Einstein's time loops. Hence a bee knows that to get from point "A" to point "B", it cannot lead through a straight direction, it has to make a curvilinear shape. While digital building of the honey comb would abstractly. On a micro scale, if taken separately a honey comb is a hexagon in shape, meaning it is formed out of six lines. The number six has significance. It is the day of the completion of the formation of earth, as most holy books indicate. If connected, the lines can form David's star. On the other hand, a bee is a soldier, a martyr, once it stings it dies. Similar to suicide attacks. Therefore there are wide implications that are embedded within the textual analysis of the Quran. Infact there are strategies that could exceed the present and the past, there are strategies of war that we used, are using and even did not reach our recognition yet. For instance, some of the Israeli soldiers in the last war went out saying that they were battling ghosts (referring to Hezbollah Guerillas). The ant in Prophet Suleiman parable was ahead of them in such technique when it advised its friends to go underground when Prophet Suleiman gathered his army of birds (maybe and God forbids, F16 planes for the Israeli Prime Minister Ihud Olmart nowadays might represent the birds gathered for Prophet Suleiman), jinni (maybe the electronic holograms and technology used by the Israeli army) and people (the present soldiers of Israel) and when he was about to invade another country (implicitly Syria or Iran or even sending a simple message to them through Lebanon's Hezbollah). Keeping in mind that the ant is a soldier after all, and in that symbolic reference, Hezbollah soldiers did develop not what president Bush described "a country within a country", but "a country under a country". For other anecdotes will further explain such timely characteristics of the Quran and other holy books parables.

Rhetoric within the *Party of God* is used through variety of books that try to explain the connection of the *Quran* and a variety of other developed materials around the same circumference of the Islamic religion and its practices. *The keys to the Heavens* is an exemplary study. The book written by

Shiekh Abbass Alkoumy (2002) and which gathers several concepts, methods, techniques and processes of praying. These methods supposedly represent systematic techniques that would organize the time of praying, for instance, before or after sunrise and sunset, night prayers, requests, prayers on the dead, prayer to bring a lost son, or thing, prayer of the hungry, prayer for healing from sickness. Such prayers combine the timing methods, *The Quran*ic verses, and holy people related to the prophet. One of the mere projections of criticism I developed as I scan the book, is that it is very much-in rhetoric-similar to Judiastic ritual of prayers. Most prayers in the book contain sorrow, agony, humiliation to the power of God, cries, etc. This is what a stereotypical image of an extreme Jew, crying on the (waling wall) "Haaet al mabkah" in Jerusalem. In many verses of the *Quran* God calls on the worshippers to call upon him, for He is near, but in none does He say cry for me, or humiliate yourselves, on the contrary God says when you praise the lord, rejoice the verses of *The Quran*. People are advised in the Quran only not to exceed in happiness because that would be harmful to the person's wisdom.

Another example, is a book written by *Abdullah* ben Mohammad ben Abbass Alzahed, and called the *Miracles of the Universe* (2001). Alzahed starts off by a worth mentioning a *Quran*ic verse of Prophet Abraham:

"This is how we show Abraham the heavens and the earth, so he will be of those of knowledge" (*The Quran,* Alanam, verse 75).

I wanted to quote the proceeding to indicate a finding in the naming of Ibrahim. Karim El-Koussa (2001) states that Abraham might be a derivative of the Canaano word Abra-om, which means the Aramean wanderer, and could be traced to Ur, a Chaldean village near Babylon (p. 102). Such wondering from the author brings to perspective that naming used to take the form of an adjective of the person's qualities, and in it there is also the indication of what the *Quran*ic verse is pointing to, which is the wander-here in the universe per-se, earth and heavens, which of course is the establisher of knowledge because it holds so much contemplation and exploration, after all Christopher Columbus did prove it through a continent or new world discovery. The book, "The Wonders of the Heavens" explicitly and implicitly projects issues of wonders in the creations and tries to explain them anthropologically, scientifically, and theologically taking a narrative methodology. Although some of the stories go beyond the sense of normal perceptions, to resemble a science fiction movie, relative stories in the book will be further discussed as we go through the chapters.

The rest of the books are scanned from the publications of The Consultative Center for Studies and Documentation from the years 1988 till 2001. Such productions as surveyed are characterized by their economical and political themes. Another publication is by the Women's Society in the *Party of God*. Various other rhetoric such as invitation cards, calendars, DVDs, photos are discussed as well. However, first things first, what is Jihad?

The Basis of Jihad

Jihad is from the verb *"Jahada"*, meaning to put effort and supplement self and society in resistance to enemies. The word in its Islamic definition is wider in its implications than its linguistic meaning as to the military fight of the enemies. It includes as well fighting the inside enemy found in every individual, which is represented through a drive towards devilish acts, the devil which calls for evil doing and everything that would lead to prevent good and promote evil (Kassem 2002, p. 44). Yet, evil is relatively defined.

Jihad is the basis in the life of every Muslim—in theory whether it is towards the self, or against the enemies. The latter is the truthful practical part of Jihad. It comes after the individual defeats all his/her material desires, so he/she would be fully capable to defeat the occupiers and wrong doers. Self-Jihad is largest, because it is a daily process and the individual is always in struggle between the good or the bad, between worshipping God and the inclination of desires. But the Jihad against enemies is the smallest, because it is only required at certain eras of the human life as a belief and value to help support the fair well of human and the nation, when the nation is put under pressure, invasion, occupation, or humiliation (Kassem 2002, p. 47).

Jihad is divided into two aspects; first-elementary or basic Jihad: Muslims start by defending the enemies, and then would invade their land not to acquire it or for defense reasons, but it is related to the prophet Mohammed, and the Imam. It is not suggested as a strategy nowadays because of the absence of Imam Mahdi (Muslims—mainly *Shai'a*—believe that an Imam, called Mahdi will show up along with Christ. Because they believe that both of them did not die yet). Second-defense Jihad: it is when Muslims defend their own land, people, selves, when they are invaded or occupied. Jihad is strictly a matter of the *"Walli"* or *Fakih*-the Muslim Leader. It is according to his rules, Muslims are not supposed to arbitrary go to war. There are rules and regulations to when Jihad is allowed (Kassem 2002, p. 51). It is set through tactics that would spoil and bring to failure any attempts to occupy, oppress, or kill Muslims.

The Western thinkers thought that this kind of sacrifice is strange. They accused the young of taking certain drugs or that their miserable life circumstances led them to such life style, other excuses is that they are exposed to certain trained behavior, or material benefit that would lead them to Jihad in their material bodies. Kassem (2002) defends military Jihad saying that the westerners are used to a materialistic mentality in explanation. Islam says it is the spiritual/religious up bringing as well as religious. Jihad is an act that needs to strive within the being first, before any persuasive stage (p. 58).

Data Collection and Analysis Procedures

After gaining access to some of the social, cultural and political activities of the *Party of God*, I managed to collect some of their rhetorical productions. Ceremonies, celebrations, events, speeches will be interpreted as rhetorical artifacts.

Specifically, this research draws upon the following:
When tackling the issue of leadership, the speeches of Nasrallah, the Secretary General of Hezbollah are compiled in (1) Bazi, M. (2004), *This is How Nasrallah Spoke.* Bazi collected speeches of Nasrallah from the year 1995 to 2004. (2) An audio tape released by *Bent Alhouda* (2004), titled *Nasrallah's Speech in the Liberation Day.* (3) Music CDs that are produced by Hezbollah called *Isra'a Band (12).*

Since *Hezbollah* is a socially, politically and economically constructed group, for every event there is a certain type of celebrations, comments, speeches, activity, book fairs, and announcements. Hence calendar events will be examined, such as the celebration of the liberation of South Lebanon, its speech and the activities will be interpreted. For instance, in order to

37

reveal diversity codes the following procedure is followed: one of the most interesting representations of the women's status, or-a simple right of enjoying a pleasurable sex life-was a silent cry sent by one of *Hezbollah* women to another through phone text-messaging. Such laugh/cry, or irony speaks of the oppression practiced in the society.

Various book fairs were visited in order to gather information and rhetorical artifacts. From these fairs a collection of books that serve in answering the dissertation questions was formed. An example of this collection would be segmented into parts; the philosophical section, such as Olleek (2004) *The Philosophy of Martydrom.* On the other hand, children's books were consulted to access the narrative style in the Arab rhetorical traditions. These books included *The Story of Karbala* (2004), and Chagall's (1999), *Arabian Nights: Four tales from a thousand and one nights.*

Narratives that are the social rhetoric, the public discourse, or the constructs of a social gossip and an emphasis of an act emerge: Gossip, talks, etc. In two of the photos, that in which portrays *Nasrallah.* The photo is supposed to be used as a sticker for the car. Slogans that are distributed for certain events, books and publications that are the out come of various events. At some point I would go there personally. Of the places that I was able to get the material were the various shopping markets that are spread in all of the Muslim *Shia'a* areas in Lebanon. There are brochures such as "The Lebanese Cultural League" that discusses women of *Hezbollah,* and their empowerment. Other philosophical books are written by authors such as Gharib (2002) *Hezbollah: Religion and politics.* Another that served in enriching the study, al-Majlisi (2003) *The Book of Occultation,* or the Series produced by the Resistant Women, such as *Bracelets from Iron,* another example would be Ya'qub (1999)

The Coneption of the Sahaba's Ultimate Decency and the Political Authority in Islam. Simply put, I followed a methodology of gathering data from the general to the particular. I would gather information that is subsequent in answering my research questions. Accordingly, I would choose parts of speech, such as Nasrallah's speech when his son died as a martyr, and would relate it to organizational constructions, such as its effects on the people, later I would relate it to the issue of martyrdom in general such as his speech or Hezbollah rhetoric of "life after death", or codes of conduct, such as Nasrallah's behavior patterns of not allowing his tears to fall on national television. These are the kinds of rhetorical moments you will witness along the study. In addition to it, I try to make sense of the concept to the non Arabic, non Islamic audience, in order to make the concept clear and the idea familiar.

Overview of Chapters

Chapter II: Rhetorical origin of the Islamic Resistance in Lebanon-the *Party of God*. It will be an introduction to the subject matter. Such investigation will be illustrated by a look from within, meaning the self presentation of the rhetoric used by the party's members in their self prologue. The rhetorical origin, the discourse created, and the discursive context. The chapter will also develop an argument and discussion of the emergence of contemporary Arabic rhetoric.

Chapter III: Diverse constructions of ethnicity, race and color trough the *Party of God* organizational structure. It will explore the rituals performed by the party. In order to interpret beliefs and behaviors of the party, and analyze its implications one of the processes I will follow is relating myth and contemporary behavior, such relationship will able to bring forth the roots of the belief system and clarify it. Through this chapter a discussion of the party's diverse constructions of ethnicity, race and color through its organizational structure and its manifestations in the Islamic religion as a whole will be explored.

40

Chapter IV: Leadership symbolic construction. It will explore the Jihad phenomena. Such explanation will explain the phenomena, its significance, and rationale. Jihad as in language, performance, myth, persuasion, reactions (national and international), and future premises will all be explored, noted and criticized. Story telling might take part in the exploration. Leadership patterns will be explained.

Chapter V: Organizational reality revealed through language codes will strictly concentrate on language patterns, codes, and practices. The organizational reality in relation to language, and performance will be investigated.

Chapter VI: Towards a better understanding of *Hezbollah* will sum up the study, stating the thesis of the dissertation.[3]

Chapter II
Rhetorical Origin of the Islamic Resistance in Lebanon

Does God Have a Party?

Chapter II discusses the origin of the Islamic Resistance. Through the analysis of the name given to it, its implications in the Arabic language, the systematic overview and development of the *Party of God* will create a primer for the chapters to follow. The chapter will also (re)present key aspects of the *Party's* history.

Israel is a name of a Prophet, most probably is that of *"Yacqub"*, Jacob who is also called Israel" (Al-Jibouri 2002, p. 255). Israel means the worshipper of God. *"Isra"* is a Hebrew word meaning worshipper, while, "El" means God. In a war for belief systems, for worship, and holy land icons among the *"Abdullahs"*, or the worshippers of God, whether from the Jewish side or that of the Muslim side, a question floats, does God have a party?

The naming of the *Party of God* has its origins in one of the verses found in the *"Quran"*:

"Your friend can be only Allah, and His messenger and those who believe, who establish worship and pay the poor due, and bow down [in prayer]. And whosoever taketh Allah and His messenger and those who believe for friends [will know that], Lo! The party of Allah, they are the victorious" (the Quran, the Table Spread; verse 56).

Meanwhile Kassem (2005) states "that the term Islamic Resistance came as an expression of an Islamic character representing firm belief in the heavenly doctrine". The *Quran* states in another Sura;

"And strive for Allah with the endeavor which is His right. He hath chosen you and hath not laid you in religion any hardship; the faith of your father Abraham [is your]. He hath named you Muslims of old time and in this [scripture] that the messenger may be a witness against you, and that ye may be witnesses against mankind. So establish worship, pay the poor due, and hold fast to Allah. He is your protecting Friend. A blessed patron and a blessed helper" (Quran, Al-hajj, 78).

This is one verse in the *"Quran"* where the *Party of God* has been mentioned. Definitely the naming has an association with the verse mentioned earlier, yet such akin is not acknowledged by some of the *Party's* members. In other words, some *Hezbollah* members interpret the verse to mean those who believe (believers) only not in particular the members, but definitely we cannot underestimate the symbolism that is meant, and the association created between the naming and the creation of the *Party of God*. A direct link associates victory with allies of the *Party of God*.

"Thought includes all the effects that have to be *Party's* by means of language; among these are proof and refutation, the awakening of emotions such as pity, fear, anger, and also exaggeration and depreciation" (Murray & Dursch 2000, p. 82). It is important to discuss two important factors here: the party (*Hezbo*) of God (*Allah*). An Arabic axiom states, *"a message can be clearly read from its title"*. In other words this is similar to metanalysis in methodological representations. The analysis here is going to take three dimensions: semantic, functional and thematic.

Concerning the rhetorical power of the name *Hezbollah*, there are many possibilities. First, it promises victory and God's support. The name also identifies people, those who are with God, and those who are not. Similar to President Bush's famous saying after September 11th attacks on New York and Washington D.C.; "You are either with us or against us". Here both sentences limit choices to an absolute dichotomy, either being with or against, or eliminates the middle ground. But it is not the last parallel within this dissertation; the political strategies of the USA and *Hezbollah* occasionally mirror one another due to strategic communication patterns under threat situations.

The rhetorical power of *Hezbollah* originates from its association with God. According to Islam, all the 99 attributes of God, I will mention a few here, are combined all in the word "Allah". Some of these attributes are the Merciful, the Peaceful, the all Knower, the Almighty, etc. Hence the sect of God, or the *Party of God* would correlate all of God's attributes under one umbrella; that of God's. Another function here is that of the word party or sect *(hezbo)* this word carries a certain distinction and categorization. It groups people, unites them, and draws them under one umbrella that of an organized group, with a legal existence, and a governmental declaration.

The rhetorical meaning of *Hezbollah* here is metaphoric. Murray & Dursch (2000) clarify, "Metaphors are the application to one thing of a name belonging to another thing, the transference maybe from the genus or from one species to another, or it maybe a matter of analogy" (p. 86). Simply put, when a person is standing in front of a library, he/she would automatically transfer the image of being a smart man/woman. Evidently clear in the transference of the *Quran*ic verse 56 and its association with victory mentioned above of *Hezbollah*, to them being victorious.

Similarly, "as an example of transference from genus to species I give "here lays my ship" for lying at anchor is a species of lying" (p. 86). And those who follow God and the prophet and they are believers, would be the *Party of God* and they would win His support transference of deed and action. Murray and Dursch (2000) point out, "for ten thousand which is a particular large number is used instead of the word many" (p. 86). They add:

"I explain metaphor by analogy as what may happen when four things the second stands in the same relationship to the first as the fourth to the third, or then one may speak of the fourth instead of the second, and the second instead of the fourth. And sometimes people will add to the metaphor a qualification appropriate to the term; which has been replaced. Thus for example, a cup stands in the same relationship to Dionysus, as a shield to Ares, and one may therefore call the cup Dionysus shield and the shield Ares' cup. Or again, old age is to life as evening is to day and so one may call the evening the old age of the day" (p. 86).

Hence, all the attributes of God mentioned earlier; are transferred to the *Party of God*, and all in the party (using metaphoric transference) shall win. Consequently the naming did serve a key movement need. It attached people to the idea of victory, and God's support. In other words, Axley (1984) states, metaphor involves "understanding and experiencing one kind of thing in terms of another. It is the symbolic representation of something in terms of something else", bringing out "the thisness of that, or the thatness of this" (p. 429). He later explains that metaphor, indeed, "is the primary means by which the formal pursuit of knowledge-science advances" (p. 429).

Murray & Dursch (2000) explain, "diction in general is made up of the following parts: the letter, the syllable, the connecting word, the conjunction, the noun, the verb, the inflexion or case, and the statement" (p. 82). The thematic dimension is not far away from the meaning of the words in *Hezbollah*. The presence of the word (*Hezbo*), which stresses the letter "Z" making it sharp once pronounced, and the ending letters of the "B" with a an enunciation of the "Woo", that would make an effect and tone of voice of "Boo". It is important to indicate that the meaning of the word "boo" in the English language is culturally and significantly different than it is in Arabic. Although it is used as to scare someone in the Western culture, "boo" in Arabic is associated with water. If asked to drink, a child would reference water as *"emboo"*. Another similar reference would be related to the patriarchal society. A father is called upon as the father of his first son's name. For instance, Johnson's father would be called "bo Johnson". Similarly, the proverb "Child is the father of man" indicates the transference of manhood state from generation to the other.

These were some associations of the pronunciation "boo", and it was very crucial to explain these differences among cultures in thematic meanings, for it all could make a difference in intercultural comprehension. While the word *Allah* would hold no comment other then the comfortable progression of the letters from A to H, which, the latter, is in its part pronounced as a sigh of relief. Through media exposure in the West, the word Allah has been associated with different meanings, and its thematic feel would elevate fear in the hearts of many Americans and Europeans. That fear is very similar to the panic and apprehension associated with *"Hezbollah"* as a party. Such association is strictly related to stereotypical presentations that are the result of political conflict which no matter how much I avoid is a crucial element in this dissertation.

But maybe a definition of the religious concept (God) would lessen the intensity of the ever-existing war of beliefs; "the word Allah" Aljibouri (2002) says "is derived from the verb *walaha* (past tense), *Yawlahu* (present tense), from the root noun *walah*. The Arabic letter "waw" was replaced with "hamza". [Walah], Aljibouri adds," is extreme love" (p. 18). Indeed, even God is associated with passion, of course the heavenly Kind. And if God is extreme love, what are the ways to reach Him? Seeking Him, human have managed various ways to get in touch with God, such as the sophistries in the West and East, and maybe Jihad or martyrdom in the Arab world. Reddy (1979) explains, metaphorical analysis can be applied to language itself, "people's conceptions and actions relative to communication are profoundly influenced by the ways they talk about it". Hence, whether subliminally or consciously, the naming of *Hezbollah* is very much referenced in the minds of people as victorious, religious, and chosen by God. In such curriculum, the Party of God is using some what a reverse psychology in its battle with the enemy. Since the Jewish claim to be the people chosen by God, *Hezbollah* exclaim that only a more sophisticated strategy would bring down the sophisticated strategy employed by the Israeli army, moreover if the latter has already offered a transfer idea and paved ground to the idea of being chosen by God.

Hezbollah developed out of various contextual circumstances; political, economical, religious and societal state of affairs. Lull (2000) cites Sowell's argument "that crucial factors in cultural formation and continuity are related largely to the social consequences of geography". He adds, "Geography is not all-determining, but it can set the limits of human possibilities narrowly or widely" (p. 153). Lull indicates:

"Internal cultural patterns reside and persist in the deep recesses of the collective consciousness and the collective memory. They are not absolute or determining, and they do not pertain to the same degree to everyone in any cultural group. They are reinforced continually through the routines of everyday life. The patterns are very resistant to change, particularly, as Sowell points out, for groups that live relatively isolated from other cultural groups" (p. 153).

However, *Hezbollah* does not live in isolation, throughout the process of its configuration, *The Party of God*, was apt and willing to mold according to various changes and shifts in politics. Throughout the coming chapters similar cultural transference will be discussed.

Ranstrope (1997), the British author of the book *"Hizb'Allah"* in Lebanon states an important point in the birth of the *Party of God*; "Prior to the organizational formation of Hizb' allah in June 1982, the Lebanese *"Shai'a"* community was largely regarded by other militias as well as outside observers, as politically irrelevant in Lebanon. This came as no surprise given the *"Shai'a"* community's historical background as socially excluded, economically deprived and politically marginalized within Lebanon, itself reinforced by the institutionalized political system of confessionalism which disadvantaged the representation of the Muslims (p. 25).

From "Origin" to Movement

Israel invaded Beirut in the year 1982. The prime reason behind the invasion was to secure its borders, and to exterminate the military structure of the Palestinian Liberation Organization (PLO)[4]. Kassem (2005) states "Beirut lived its toughest, most grueling days under destructive Israeli aerial bombardment. The capital's numerous points of entry fell under siege, supplies grew scarce; life came to halt, a great number of people were displaced, died or were injured and many buildings came down on those on it " (p. 88). The same strategy was repeatedly implemented in the recent "open war" of July 2006. Hereby the Israeli army and Hezbollah as well as the Lebanese and Israeli public are taking some types of precautions, either by changing their battle tactics, allowing a more engagement of the UN, or simply by building shelters under each new building!

During that time and similarly now, every family had a story to tell about the vulgarity of war. Mr. Afif Kodeeh, a friend of my family is a perfect example of such tragedies occurring at that time. Kodeeh lost his whole family in the 1982 invasion. After leaving the building to buy food for his family, he returned back to find that he lost his wife, his three kids and some neighbors. Later on, Koddeh started new, he remarried, and formed a new family. Perhaps anecdotal, however this is example of how the Lebanese character will survive and adapt. Hence, part of that adaptation to the new political, militarized context was the formation of *Hezbollah*. And it will also continue as a transition and evolution of war characteristics from generation to generation embedded with specific modifications.

While the Lebanese interpreted Hezbollah as a response to the invasion by Israel, Ranstorp (1997) advances an alternative interpretation held by the West. He indicates that not only the Lebanese context was ready for the *Party of God's* birth process but also "subsequently, the emergence of Hizb 'allah in 1982 was perceived by the West largely within the context of Iran's revolutionary efforts to export its revolution following Israel's 1982 invasion of Lebanon" (p. 25). And what better ground would be other than the *Shia'a* who as mentioned earlier was overshadowed in Lebanon. However, Ranstrop adds that "although recognizing that Iran played a decisive role in the emergence of Hizb 'allah, from being initially a small group spread headed by senior *Shia'a* clergy without a distinct organizational apparatus to a full-fledged participant in the mainstream of Lebanese politics, the political mobilization of Lebanon's *Shia'a* community has occurred in stages which preceded the Islamic revolution in Iran and Hizb 'allah's entry as a radical and militant organization in June 1982 by several decades" (p. 25). Yet, the author fails to mention the transformation occurring from since the liberation of South Lebanon in the year 2000 in the politics of the *Party of God*. Such failure is due to the year of publication, and the author's emphasis on the hostages' abduction. For instance, the Iranian support for an Islamic Revolution to more materialistic support (other than weapon wise) such as building a hospital (Sheikh Ragheb Hareb) in South Lebanon, under the supervision of Iranian management. These changes also carried an ideological conversion. Meanwhile, the Secretary General of Hezbollah in an interview made with Assafir newspaper clearly declares that "the people will someday realize that *Hezbollah* is the most politically free movement".

"The coastal boulevard and the *Western Bekaa*, operations which were crowned by the first martyrdom attack executed by *Ahmad Kassir* on November 11, 1982 and targeting the headquarters of the Israeli command in Tyre, South Lebanon. This operation shook Israel like a tremor" (Kassem 2005, p. 89). Although, it was not mentioned at that time how *Hezbollah* was subsidized with armory and weapons [doubts would solely be pointed towards Iran and recently USSR]. Nevertheless, at some point it raises some doubt that a mere announcement from "the Jurist-Theologian Imam Khomeini declared: *"Israel is a cancerous gland"*. As such, *Hezbollah* rose to this target and launched Islamic resistance operations against Israel with whatever limited numbers of individuals and capabilities were available" (p. 67), trying to exterminate the cancerous cell and restore Lebanon's healthy system.

Ranstorp (1997) states three stages in the establishment and expansion of the *Party of God*. "The establishment of Hizb'allah, with active Iranian supervision, in Lebanon occurred in three phases and the movement divided its operations into three main geographical areas: the Biqa'a, Beirut, and the South. Each of these regional divisions were lead by high-ranking Hizb'allah clergy with local background and affiliation to a network of loyal supporters" (p. 34).

Again, the active Israeli invasion of Lebanon *Party's* a reaction [the training camps set up in the Bekaa area and supervised by the Iranian Islamic Revolutionary Guard constituted the primary source of resistance fighters or *mujahideen* for the Islamic Resistance. These camps were also the source of information for cultural, spiritual, behavioral and jihad qualities, all of which were essential traits in the personalities of revolutionary guard members (p. 67).

The first appearance of *Hezbollah* members was in secrecy and silence, "Resistance fighters worked in secret circles without any political or media appearances" (p. 68). However, that political and military movement was supplemented by a need a social, economic, and public need among the *"Shia'a"* sect for a voice in Lebanon. *"Shia'a"* sects were marginalized groups *Hezbollah*'s presence came to be a release to the tension created by decades of discriminations. Ranstorp (1997) states that "immediately following Israel's invasion, Iran urged Syria to allow the deployment of a small Iranian contingent into Lebanon and also to turn the war in Lebanon into a religious war against Israel" (p. 34).

Concerning that of the political dimension, it is clearly stated by Kassem (2005) that Israel was the primary reason; "the core objective of the Israel's 1982 invasion of Lebanon was to annihilate the military structure of the Palestine Liberation Organization (PLO)" (p. 87). Thus through such invasion Israel had in its tactics that this would secure the borders. A web of strategies that would make the invasion looks like an act of defense rather than an aggression. Kassem (2005) affirms "during those rapid and successive events, resistance groups had started formation, executing more than one military operation against the occupation forces in Beirut" (p. 89). Therefore, one could metaphorically state that the Israeli's invasion of Lebanon was born along a twin brother, *Hezbollah* (action and reaction). Conversely, there were other family members in the sphere; certain types of escalations arose because of the presence of the Palestinian camps in Beirut "*Hezbollah* suffered the discontent of its family of supporters as a result of the tense relations between the Palestinians and the *"Shia'as"* existing prior to the Israeli invasion" (p.100). However, direct Syrian sponsorship had an effect in stabilizing the situation according to *Hezbollah's* concepts. After the Palestinian-*Hezbollah* escalation, this could be summed as that of a Sunni, *"Shia'a"* conflict, there arose a different type of conflict that of *"Shia'a"* vs. *"Shia'a"* clash. Kassem (2005) explains "working on one front, *Party's* of the *Amal* and *Hezbollah* factions interacted as one family, the sharing of experience becoming the bread and butter between these brothers of the same household and sons of the same village" (p. 101), however the sweet turned to be bitter at a certain period of clash between the two fractions. The competitive atmosphere in recruitment was not the only reason that led both *Parties* to conflict for sometime "added to this was the breach of trust between the two *Parties* resulting from the interpretation of major issues on various political stances, and a conflict ensued leading to a tragic series of clashes, a black page in history" (p. 101). Indeed it was because the election campaigns for the board of representatives in the year 2005 joined the two fractions in one list.

Another turn in *Hezbollah's* evolution was that of the "Taif Accord". Kassem (2005) states, "the internal Lebanese environment was not in any better state than the battlefront. Civil war and the Israeli invasion had taken their toll on the population, fragmenting and segregating East from West Beirut-or in broader terms, Muslims from Christians, as per the prevailing sectarian and geographic distribution" (p. 103).

The word *"Taif"* in this sense means sect. In order to settle the inside conflict that was taking place at that point, "efforts at the Taif meetings in Saudi Arabia focused on constitutional amendments tackling political organizational setup, the authority of the three main heads of state, and alterations to the constitution that had a bearing on sectarian specifics" (p. 103). *Hezbollah* had their own comments on the accord, overall, it was "not convincing and below the minimum required" (p.104). Some believed that this discontent was due to the conflict between the two *"Shia'a"* fractions. "However, some resorted to linking the Amal /Hizbullah conflict in the South which still raged after the accord, to *Hezbollah's* attempt at rupturing the Taif Accord and using the situation in the South as a pretext" (p. 104). "The approach chosen by *Hezbollah* in its objection to the nature and structure of the confessional regime in Lebanon was the correct political approach in expressing political positions" (p. 104).

Moreover, the presence of the Lebanese government lead to a chain of events related to the legal structure of *Hezbollah*. On top of it is that of its armory and weapons, later on its political format and contributions. These issues are being solved and negotiated according to several laws, "Given the party's priority for resistance activity, the nonintervention guarantees received through Syria, the changed political direction and the army's function, and Syrian guidance over these developments, *Hezbollah* decided to respond positively to the "Greater Beirut" project whereby the army would take custody of security over the capital and its suburbs" (p. 105).

The subject of disarmament is commented upon by Kassem (2005) as follows:

> "This development originated in the party's vision of refusing a government within-a-government. It was also an element of the party's methodical frame of mind to forbid the use of weapons by Party members for any internal balance or control purposes under the umbrella of an existing government otherwise such use would only lead to antagonism and internal

dissension. Given that the requirement is to preserve the Party's resistance function, there was no need for maintaining armaments outside vicinity, especially given a political atmosphere supportive to the Resistance and of protection to its back ranks. As for the continuing danger facing the leaders of the Resistance wherever they were, this was dealt with in cooperation with the relevant security organizations, through providing them with arms-bearing licenses within the limits of use for personal protection against any Israeli breach security" (p. 105).

Indeed, *Hezbollah*'s weapons have not been used outside the Lebanese/Israeli conflict, nor inside Lebanon. However, such argument stems towards the *Party of God*'s organization. Internal organization was unavoidable, created out of a need, such organization developed to be the best organized Party in Lebanon. The following discussion would reveal these crucial facts. Kassem (2005) states, "a hierarchical pyramid structure was finally adopted as the Party's organizational formula" (p. 60). Such formula was established after sometime of chaotic fundamentals resulting from a trial to set theory into practice.

The first issue that surfaced in the construction was that of membership; "Entitlement to Party membership was conferred upon those who adopted the Party's goals in their entirety, committed to Party organizational directives, agreed to the time limit projected for the Party to undertake its functions, and possessed general personal, religious belief, behavioral and jihad credentials which qualified them for entering the system and for growing within it while undertaking their obligations" (Kassem 2005, p.60). The process that is being developed here is similar to any organizational context within institutional framework. However, organization not only entails a process of labor, effort and production but as well socialization. Identification not only serves in increasing the attachment and loyalty with the organization, but it also allows for a conglomeration between the self of the employee and the organizational community. In short, the end task would be thinking of self as thinking of organization. Such process is not fully accomplished under any circumstances, later on ground demonstrations in the organizational frame of the *Party of God* would pertain at some point new amendments, reformations, partition etc., which as well demonstrate the practical spirit of organization.

Such organization did not take a formal shape where an Identification card would be presented, or distributed, but in the contrary it counted on a structure similar to surveying people; "no membership tokens were distributed, as affiliates were not the only individuals contributing to the Party's goals. The definition of affiliation to the Party was not tied to a Party identification card" (Kassem 2005, p. 60). However, their are certain distinct behavior patterns among the people affiliated with Hezbollah.

Such organizational behavior is a two-way strategy, on one hand, it opens the options of membership via anonymous belonging especially when it was risky to belong to *Hezbollah*. However, that same issue of belonging is on stake here, because identification is not certificated. Moreover, such strategy would minimize what Deetz (2001) discusses "centrality of codification, the search for regularity, and normalization, and the implied prescriptive claim" (p. 19).

Ranstorp (1997) states that in Beirut "Hizb'allah's natural source for organizing Shi'ites was to work within the framework of existing radical Shi'ite organizations and religious institutions" (p. 36). Ranstorp adds;

"Part from recruiting more fundamentalist elements within Amal, who followed the example set by the departure of Husayn al-Musawi and Sheikh Ibrahim al-Amin, the involvement of Shiekh Muhammad Hussein Fadlallah proved to be important for Hizb 'allah as he commanded a considerable number of Shi'a followers in the Bir al-Abed quarters of southern Beirut, through his activity in the mosque of al-Sallum. Arriving from Najaf to Beirut in 1966, Shiekh Faddlallah's high-ranking religious stature was due both to his longstanding charitable work among poor urban Shi'ite community, who arrived from southern Lebanon and the Biq 'a, as well as to his preaching and writings, in which he advocated political activism and force as a means to preserve and defend Islam in favor of traditional Shi'ite policy of quietism and dissimulation" (p. 37).

"Individuals were required to observe and comply with their assigned Party functions, the most important of which was resistance activity" (Kassem 2005, p.60), such plan requires coordination. Put simply, there is a state of functional tradition taking place here, Burrell and Morgan (1979) state that functionalism represents a perspective which is firmly rooted in the sociology of regulation, approaches its subject matter from an objectivist point of view" (p. 25). Hence, "making available the appropriate job description frame work was another Party priority, along side the distribution of functional responsibilities and authority boundaries needed for effective goal execution and facilitation of coordination among the Party's various units" (Kassem 2005, p.60).

In order to establish a social ground, "a broad recruitment process was launched across the various districts and villages, one encompassing all those interested in joining the Party", although the nature of such recruitment is not fundamentally clear in nature or the public relations strategies used to recruit. However, such strategy is evident in distributing brochures, or yearly calendars, where events, lectures, Islamic dates of significance, photos of the armories *Hezbollah* purchases, the Secretary General, or/and martyr's photos. "The hierarchical management of these recruits was based on district demographics and geographic distribution. *Party's* was a function of individual circumstances and time availability. All affiliates took part in military and cultural training, combat and post guardianship, as well as any general functions required by the Party" (Kassem 2005, p.60).

Women are not far from the public work. On the contrary, the women's role among *Party of God* is very crucial and vital. There are women writers, very well educated, and dedicate their social work in literary production, there are women soldiers, or fighters, which was one of the first roles adopted in their society-after Iran. Hence, in general there has been no role that was not adopted by women. Kassem (2005) states "Women's societies were created, and roles distributed throughout mosques and districts. The objective was to achieve cultural and societal recruitment to the end of securing a presence in the activities and general call for the Party" (p.60). For instance, cards on mother's days, in April 2005, where distributed to all families, with the sponsorship of *Hezbollah*, what was striking in those cards is that they adopted the feminist colors used in the USA, purple, as their design plan!

In addition to women's cause that are granted a great contribution in the organizational hierarchy, youngsters, have their own manifestos as well. Kassem, explains; "Youth recruitment and cultivation was channeled through founding the Imam al-Mahdi Scouts, where alongside general part in the Party's broad undertakings, activities that were in harmony with the young generation's needs were planned" (p.60). Summer camps where children get a chance to train intellectually and physically. The intellectual training would involve religious upbringing such as memorizing the *Quran*, competitions and prizes among kids. It will also contain various activities such as computer training. Computer games are at some point exclusive of *Hezbollah* where a game would detail a military combat done against Israeli soldiers.

In conclusion, this was an overview of the rhetorical origin of the *Party of God*. There are other aspects of organization that takes place in here, some of these aspects are mentioned in Gharyeb (2002) book; *Hezbollah: Religion and Politics,* where she discuses the opposition of the *Party of God* to the Western culture. The author mentions that the *Party of God* defines their opposition is circled around political issues. The main ideological issue is the despise *Hezbollah* holds towards the materialism that envelops the brutal capital society of the West (p. 120).

Moreover, another comment which the author points out, that of the superiority that the Western societies hold towards what it labels "third world countries". The way the western media describes the west as being an ideal place for order, while, portraying the third world countries as the ideal place for chaos (p. 120). This, topped with stereotypical images of the Muslims in Western media as villains and advocating for Israeli interests in the area, all contributed to the escalated state of affairs between the West and the Muslim east, and in particular the *Party of God*.

Chapter III
Organizational Structure and
Diverse Constructions of *Hezbollah*

Civil Rights: A Renewed Trend

When discussing *Hezbollah* as an Islamic Resistance and movement, the following argument will make clear, how it is a movement of diverse constructs within its hierarchal structure. Concerning race, ethnicity, diversity, feminism and other constructs included in the organizational system, Hezbollah is a renewed trend. This chapter addresses the second research question: How does the *Party of God* mediate and accommodate its diverse organizational structure.

Just like a new trend of clothing, the West or the trading company expects the East, or the consumer to adopt quickly, disregarding naturalization procedures. At such stance, underdeveloped countries would have to adopt social institutions and social values resembling those of the West. In here, I suggest a form of neo-orientalism that surpasses Edward Said's descriptions of the West's thoughts and East's behaviors and image, a neo-orientalism that would radicalize Arab identity by resisting Zionist and Western hegemony. Said explained how the West views the East. Neo-orientalism will allow the East to define itself rather than be defined, and to explain its processes rather than having it forced and channeled. For instance, this is what the Lebanese prime minister tried doing when his ministry backed the "Seven Points Plan" that draws a resolution to the end of the " open war" of July 2006. Within this radicalized identity there is a place for the orient Said described, yet rhetorically accomplishes a new acceptance and understanding. For instance, Garrett (1999) states "orientalism need not manifest itself so starkly to have pernicious effects. Starting from the assumption that the other is an *other*- is different, exotic, mysterious, and strange the scholar may gravitate toward what seems most different, exotic, mysterious, and strange in the other culture" (p. 58).

Indeed, such portrayal would move towards not depriving the exotic from the East, but rather allowing its emergence at the two sides of the coin, the East and the West; the emergence of exotic diversity, to think of it as something we know rather than ignore, and to change the attitude towards the word exotic from the suspense to the comfort of practice. It is a step the Islamic East did not take yet, but needs an encouragement. And the West is very busy in solving the East's puzzles and labyrinths to allow its emergence. Until that time, I would like the Western audience to consider that the East as well considers it the *other*, the exotic, the mysterious and the strange at some standards, regardless of the continuous Western media exposure and interaction (whether military or civilian). To some Eastern or in particular Muslim societies the West is the orient. So for the others, those who speak in simple sentences, and are clear, not mysterious, and linear in form, and communication, I invite them to a neo-oriental presentation, they are part of not in geography but in culture, to understand when spoken to in a curvilinear structure, to respond when addressed in some "strange" behavior such as not shaking hands as a salutation but rather bowing down; hence, culture will surpass borders to become intercultural communication.

Taking narratives into consideration, Arab famous integrity and honored history beholds a whole load of civil rights developments. A long time ago, before that Western revolution to implement a diverse society and to appreciate its presence, there came Islam with visions of equality and the narratives that advocate for it are plenty; among them is the famous saying of Prophet Muhammad (Peace Be Upon Him).

The Prophet was against slavery, and discrimination according to race, color and ethnicity, for another famous narrative is that of *Bilal*, a black African who was considered a slave. His task was to go and call for the prayers in the high building of what later on became known as a mosque. The call, which still is practiced nowadays, is a narrative that calls for good work, good prayer, and that unifies the belief to one God. *Bilal*, at the time of the prophet reminds me so much of some African American singers and rappers, in the USA now who gained their freedom through a medium.

Although of these singers might be "rapping" or "gospelling" yet, the scenery is similar while at some point, the scenario might differ. But *Bilal*, and taken as a stereotypical image of the freedom given through lyrics and out loud prayer, so was the freedom in the USA for some African Americans, and Hispanics, who at some point form a heavy mass of the pop culture in the USA.

However, if freedom is measured by the amount of words

uttered, the following joke would make sense in revealing how much oppression is subjected over the women of Hezbollah. Women of *Hezbollah*, do not enjoy the same rights as the American society practices or reinforces in the civil rights movements. Here, stereotypes serve as model types. Examining real situations comes shocking no matter how much advocating and promotion for deconstruction, acquired performances of race and affiliates. Yet, one of the most interesting representations of the women's status, or simple rights of enjoying a pleasurable sex life was a silent cry sent by one of the *Hezbollah* women to another through phone messaging. Such laugh/cry, or irony speaks loud of the oppression committed upon the society of the Arab world as a whole and says:

What do women say when they are having Sex?

American: Yeah, Yeah.

German: More, more.

British: Oh, yes!

French: Plus fort.

Lebanese: Don't tell anybody, please.

This was a joke told by a *Sheikh's* wife. A laugh, but embedded with a cry. Is it a call for liberation (embedded by various meanings of liberty)? Not completely. For that issue will be tackled through various arguments discussed and initiated mainly by Fadlullah, who was one of the organizers of *Hezbollah*. Whether it is a cry, for free open sexual expression or not, it sure is not a joke!

There is a hidden intense feeling about sexual denials within the Arab society in general and that is embedded within Hezbollah's social behaviors. However, there are various intertwined fabrics that come into play within the Arabic context that does not allow any behavior to be fully copied from the West, nor I claim that it should be.

Hence, when tackling the issue of diversity and its portrayal with in *Hezbollah*'s organization, I shall start with Islamic/ Arabic beliefs and traditions. "Women do not reach high status within the organization of *Hezbollah*" a professor confessed, proving my note of the organizational structure, where gospels, religious lectures, and various other activities are performed by men within the diverse society including both men and women. But women live in another section of Hezbollah's world, literally said. They have their meetings, their hierarchical structure among themselves. They even pray behind men, whenever they are together in order not to allow any sexual thoughts or temptations. However, that structure just makes me wonder, don't they consider the women's feelings, for they as well are subject to temptation!

The lines of *Hezbollah* are set, some of them are drawn by men, and among the most famous Sheikh's that discussed women's issues was Fadllulah, who also published books of such descriptions. After summarizing Islamic beliefs, I will start by describing women's dress code, for it does form a big controversy within the Western world, and we heard that the Islamic Cover was banned in France's universities and official offices, where by contrast, the USA, by law admits the freedom of belief and practice while socially it sets some limits over the way this should be practiced.

Islamic Beliefs

Pre-Islamic customs and traditions that may be of pagan origin are given religious sanctions. Perhaps the most noteworthy of this is the *Kaaba*, the meteorite black stone located in Mecca which has assumed a central position in the

Islamic pilgrimage ritual even though it was revered by local pre-Islamic pagan tribes from pre-historic times. According to Muslim tradition, the *Kaaba* was originally built by Adam as the house of God and was rebuilt by Abraham with *Ismael's* help after it was destroyed by the flood. The existence of sects and divisions within Islam, while of great importance from the standpoint of regional diversities in social and cultural patterns, does not distract from the significant cultural homogeneity with which religion endows Islamic societies

The actual unity of Islam was, in fact, disrupted very early in its history by the conflict over the succession of the Calipha from the Arabic word Khalifa (meaning successor) shortly after the death of Mohammed. This issue led to the schism out of which emerged the great division within Islam, the Sunni (followers of the tradition) and the Shi'a (followers of Ali). It also set a precedent for further divisions in later generations. The difference between Sunnis and the Shias are not primarily theological. Shiaism originated as an Arab political movement to restore the house of Ali to the Caliphate and took on many aspects of a lower class revolt against the ruling Sunni hierarchy.

It is important to mention the brief history about the Arabs, for although the *Hezbollah* movement is associated or influenced by Iran (as commonsense from media suggests), it has common grounds with the Arabs in general as well. Hence to study *Hezbollah* also requires a small review of the Arab world.

The Arab world refers to the twenty-one Arab countries that cover vast territories extending from the African shores of the Atlantic Ocean to the Arab/Persian Gulf in Asia (Ameri &Rami, p. 1). These countries are members of a League, called the Arab League, which was founded in the year 1945 but never practiced a unified identity! However the history of the Arabs goes a long way back before the World War II agreement, that resulted in forming the Arab world map as identified-or fought to be identified- as constructed nowadays. This agreement came as a result of the Balfour Declaration, Friedman (1989) defines it as the "declaration issued by British Foreign Secretary Arthur J. Balfour, endorsing the idea of establishing a 'national home' for the Jewish people in Palestine" (p. xi).

Learning that many of the world's civilizations evolved in the Arab world, such as the Babylonian Empire, made me proud. Knowing that it created one of the first legal systems with written laws, the Hamurabi Code, made me feel secure within an environment of civil war and war with Israel. And hearing that the Nile River was the center for the empires of the pharaohs, the Egyptian kings, watered my thirst. In addition to the proceeding bits of information, I felt particularly proud of the Phoenician Empires that were centers for flourishing civilizations based on trade and commerce. The Phoenicians created one of the first written alphabets, the teachers would explain. My ancestors were present in past civilizations. Yet, that was half of the truth. Among the history lessons, the present contradicted the past. We were empires in the past, now we are ruins of many empires. We exported knowledge and enlightenment, now we are importing schools and missionaries from the West. Yet the Islamic religion teacher came once a week to teach us, he was very polite, unlike other teachers he never yelled, even if he caught us cheating. What is Islam? Who are *Hezbollah*? And why did my cousin join them? Why are we fighting Israel? These were some of the questions pounding in my brain as I stepped from the elementary division to the intermediate.

According to the Muslim faith, by 610 A.D. the Prophet

Mohammad, a merchant in the city of Mecca, began to receive revelations from Allah the Arabic word for God, these revelations were written down in the Qur 'an the Muslim holy book, and became the foundation of Islam, the religion teacher explains. Within a few decades, the majority of the Arabs in the Arabian Peninsula had converted to Islam. Although conquered people in earlier empires had been forced to convert to the religious and practices of the ruling power, the Arabs did not force people to convert to Islam (Ameri & Rami, p. 13). Under Islamic law, "people of the book" Jews and Christians could not be forced to convert. They also did not serve in the military, but they did have to pay an additional tax.

From 650 A.D. to 750 A.D. the vast Arab/Islamic Empire was ruled by the Umayyad Caliphate which took Damascus as their capital of the empire. The Ummayyad dynasty was overthrown by the Abbasid Caliphs, named after Abbes, the first Caliph in the dynasty or line of rulers (Ameri & Rami, p. 14). The Abbasid took Baghdad as their capital and was known as the City of Peace. Baghdad, "City of Peace" in the Islamic world as we learned in class, was contradicted by the news I heard from the television at home, where "Bombs over Baghdad" was not only a song American citizens danced to in the USA, but also a reality that shook children from their bed, and starved families for over a decade now Iraq. The Abbasid Empire reached the peak of its power under Caliph Harun al-Rachid, another past/present contradictory figure.

Harun al-Rachid, my father exclaims, he has heard many stories about him other than those found in *One Thousand and One Nights*, stories that have been transferred from generation to generation. My father used to work as a barber in his father's shop when he was a teenager, and people when they hand their head to the barber they as well hand all the information in it.

Luckily, my uneducated father had sophisticated customers that entertained his job, and compensated his love for knowledge. "He talked to the cloud, saying, go, you cloud anywhere, you wish and desire in the sky, for where ever you choose to stop and rain, it is going to be my land" my father adds. "He was very arrogant, look where the Shi 'a Muslims are nowadays, down in the drain" he nods his head (as he rhymes his words the way he heard them). Harun al-Rachid, masked sometimes as Shahrayar, the masculine ruler with a virgin bride complex. Thank god he was not present in Judith Butler 's age, nor Simone de Beauvoir, or maybe he is, I sometimes see him reincarnated in my brother 's performative acts. Anywise, what have both scholars done that Scheherazade, didn 't do? They all told a tale, performed an act and convinced the subject matter (masculine figure) to preserve their lives, and maybe enhance their position, but Scheherazade's position in comparison to contemporary feminists was a way better than any woman nowadays, at least she was able to manage a "communicator-storyteller-historian" job and being a mother of the king 's two children, adding to that in Lebanon, a freedom that does not end in a car explosion.

But whether portrayed with a bomb or without, Arabs were intelligent scholars as well, they became world famous for their work in the sciences, particularly astronomy geometry, and in medicine. The major contributions of Arab scholars included the use of zero, the identification and naming of many star constellations, and the advances in the fields of navigation, optics (the science that deals with light), and medical care (Ameri & Rami, p. 14). Muslim artists were known for their use of decorative geometric patterns and Arabesque (ornate design of intertwined vines, leaves, and flowers). A comparison between the Arabs before Islam and after would make the picture clearer of how Islam contributed to the life of Arabs. Arabs before Islam, were nomads. They were living in tents, dirty, worshipping stone, burying girls alive, slaving and beslaved. Even the name of the tribe Mohammad belonged to was *"Kouraish"* which if translated to English can mean a small shark (or a small amount of money). This can make sense and can as well project a picture of how survival was in a dark sea of savages, and much more significance to the evolution process if I mentioned the fact that the Middle East and part of Europe used to be a sea, all covered with water, before any records of history (or if there is a completely capitalist society, hungry for money till the last penny). Thus Islam to that dark era was compared to the enlightenment to medieval Europe.

Pleasure Code

However, since justice (in *Hezbollah's* measurement) was partially accomplished so far in South Lebanon, the "Islamic Resistance", has been enjoying a shift in attitudes. From their concentration on Jihad, which is still an available resource, the Islamic Resistance shift in attitudes has been regarded in social, economic as well as political standards.

From a social perspective, the rise of the Muslim sect has brought liberation to Muslim *"Shia'a"* in social aspects in addition to the liberation of the land. For instance, they have developed a code of marriage that is similar to the boyfriend/ girlfriend structure of the western civilization, yet organized to secure the rights of women as well as men. This type of marriage is called "Pleasure Marriage", and submits to certain rules and regulations, but its main origin is to lessen the sexual suppression of religion, and to fit the sexual needs of the society.

Due to Jihad, many families, wives and children lost their husbands, fathers, or sons. The original development of *pleasure marriage* was to the wives of the martyrs who instead of suffering the loss, and having to spend the rest of their lives as widows, can get compensated by an assigned husband, who belongs to the Islamic Resistance. The marriage does not have to be officially registered; however, they get to sign an internal agreement that secures the rights of the wife in case of pregnancy and economical support. Hence the martyr would know that his wife and children would be in safe hands after his/her departure. Meanwhile organizations have as well developed a support means to the families of the martyrs in case they did not have any sponsorship. These are descriptions where Hezbollah performances within the society are described and analyzed. Fadllulah is one of the major religious leaders who tackled women's issues. But, Fadllulah is not associated with Hezbollah anymore. Hence, one of the methods that were followed in data collection here is the simple act of observation.

However, later on pleasure marriage was extended to reach a wider population. It was not only restricted to widows. Women, who passed eighteen years old, with the approval of their families, are permitted to sign a pleasure marriage contract. The reason behind this acceptance is to lessen the firmness of the religion, prevent adultery, and practice safe sex under the guidance of God. On top of it all it is considered respectful to the women's body. The whole concept requires the women to admit to the man that under God's eye she agrees to marry him, she can ask for an amount of money or other material things as an exchange of that marriage. It is enough to say the words verbally, "I allow you to marry me", however, it is suggested to sign an internal agreement between the two, suggesting that the man would take care of the women, socially by adopting the offspring, and economically, by financial support in case of need. (and if she gets pregnant while they are under the oath). Hence, the two would be safe from societal harm, and on top of it all, from disobeying God. Pleasure marriage allows individuals to practice their humanity rather than acting under their animal instincts. However it affirms the recognition of a superior power, that of God. This program shows a respect to the body, the container of the soul. It also is recognition to the human rights in enjoying the senses God granted the human in a respectful dignified manner.

In the summer of 2005, I was surprised to hear that my friend's father died of a heart attack. However my surprise was bigger when people started talking about him having another wife. "He married her in a pleasure marriage contract" my mother said. And it was only after his death when the whole family found out. "She went up to them, during the funeral, saying that she has the same right to accept condolences, and when the family asked what gives her the right, she pulled out a paper saying that she was his wife," my mother adds. "They had to take the first wife to the hospital after she fainted upon hearing the news, and now the second wife is asking for her right in his inheritance," my mother sums up.

There are many stories similar to that narrative. Pleasure marriage has evolved from being a social solution to a social problem. Some would claim that it is their right and it protects against adultery, and a proper way to balance the exceeding women numbers over men. While others would claim that it is a social problem and destruction to the family life. However, this type of marriage is dependent on the social and economic structure of the families. People with lower social and economic class would accept their daughter to perform such type of marriage so they can enhance their social status at some point. However, it is still suggested that the standard relationship of a man and woman to be joined in a scared matrimony as the primary performance of joining the two people, however, alternatives could always serve special cases, such as these mentioned earlier.

Dress Code

Another social shift in the cultural practices centered on dressing codes. Before the Liberation of South Lebanon, members of the Islamic Resistance Group were bonded to certain dress codes. Men had to dress, mainly in black, with the shirt put on top the pants. An individual could identify the political affiliation of another individual to *Hezbollah* through that dress code. Moreover, men had as well to grow their beards and mustache. Yet, they do shape the beard unlike the strict Hebrew faith who just let it grow naturally. After the liberation of South Lebanon, supporters of the Islamic Resistance Group were no longer bound to such dress code. Members started wearing colors, although it was still preferable to have the shirt on top of the pants, for decency reasons, because pants outline sex organs. This cultural practice is similar to those of the Arabian white *"Abayia"*, to the Jewish black religious dress, and the Scottish kilt. However, *Hezbollah* places such behavior in a moral context. Sexual organs would distract attention within an organizational community. In order to limit the unconscious and the conscious from elaborating on sexual fantasies, that is only allowed within the previously discussed marriage arrangement, and "since Adam and Eve descended to earth and God showed them their *"Aowra"* meaning body organs with sexual reference, inspiring them to cover with fig tree leaves", hence clothing should be a respectful behavior to the self and the surrounding community. A researcher would argue that this might be a double-edged sword. Covering would only increase fantasies, but would decrease seduction. And that covering, in the male 's case, is not limited to the sexual organs, for many people (considering fetishism) has variable attractions other than the sexual organs, such as the chest, the arms, the legs, etc.

As for women, it is required that they wear a cover-veil. Before the Liberation of South Lebanon, this cover was strictly black, and from head to toe. It is argued that such dress code liberates women more than it restricts them. First, they are easy to put on, thus saving time in choosing what to wear. Second they are financially affordable, efficient, and allow all members of the society to be and look equal. Third, they reduce sexual fantasies and seductions, and disregard the women as a mere sexual object. These explanations behold double standards as well. Equality is not only in looks. For other material implications such as the car, the house and other possessions can indicate the social level of the individual. Concerning seduction, harassment cases were as well filed from women who wear covers. Moreover, it causes the formation of a suppressed generation and the alienation of feelings between the sexes.

Yet the black cover evolved, with the involvement of women in work and organizational life to a long dress called *"althoub alshareaha"* with a head cover. After the liberation, women were allowed to wear colored veils, fashioned as well with regular dresses that would cover their chest, arms and ankles. The reason behind such shifts in women 's dressing codes is that many families, who were not actively involved with *Hezbollah* before the liberation of South Lebanon, joined

Hezbollah after the liberation, and these women were culturally open and liberal, they would wear a veil because they believed that it is descent, disciplinary, and a social as well as environmental protection to them, a means to fit in with the culture. However, older women still prefer the traditional style of dress.

Celebration Code

Before the Liberation of South Lebanon, social gatherings would be to ensure religion, and social services, as well as to encourage nationalism towards a Lebanese identity, and Lebanese liberation. Celebrations were held to strengthen the faith towards the goals and beliefs of *Hezbollah*, and the Islamic religion. Celebrations were not occasions of happiness and joy. They were calendar based, with the ultimate happy experience was the birth of the prophet Mohammed where religious songs would be played, candles lit, women separated from men rejoice in their own "womanish" way, where they get to take off their veil, dress up, get to know each other, look for brides for their sons, and eat special food prepared for the event. Men's celebrations, on the other hand were politically based. Among men religious affirmation of sacrifice, and patience, as well as education and information would be exchanged. People were happy to return to their homelands. They felt secure, under the protection of the newly liberated South Lebanon. And they felt secure that there was a chance that they can live peacefully. At a certain period of time before the Liberation, "Islamic Resistance" changed its name to be "Lebanese Resistance". It opened to all Lebanon and all Lebanese from various sects and factions. But the support varied morally, politically, financially and socially. The Lebanese men committed to the Resistance did take a chance to secure a better future, retain the land and secure it. The main concept that they emphasize was the right of the Lebanese people to have their land and restore human rights to the civilians of the area. Celebrations after the liberation were in three forms. One form would be for women, organized to eat, dance and reassure their affiliation. This gathering would be organized by the Women's Center of *Hezbollah*. Women would act free, inside the hall they would take off their veils, dance and discuss the culture, emphasize the role of the "people of the house", meaning Mohammed's family. The second form of celebration is for men only; they would be gathering to discuss politics, religion, and religious songs. The third form, which is strictly political and would combine both men and women. This kind of celebration would either be a memorial to the martyrs, or for religious and political speeches. These types of celebrations are usually open to the public.

Conclusion

The preceding codes; dress, celebration, and marriage, constitute the organizational structure of Hezbollah-as it extends into the border Lebanese society. In order to retrieve a familiar rhetoric to the readers, such practices were described, analyzed and at some point signified the organizational structure in concept and construction.

Culture produces and conveys common knowledge over time. All the material that we have been preserving from the past such as scripts, text, ruins, architecture, laws and regulations· are conveyors of common sense and knowledge (Philipsen 1992). Since that is the case, what would also survive to the generations to come is as well what we leave as common sense. It is rarely that we would hear, read or view issues that are not common sense (or constructed with common values), for the later belongs to the public, and the public has always managed to achieve a sense of permanence. It is only those who are scattered, that get to be erased like the sand drawings on the beach. In other words, "culture,…refers to a *socially constructed and historically transmitted pattern of symbols, meanings, premises, and rules*" (Philipsen 1992, p. 7, emphasis in original).

Language use is an example of common sense transference. Words and languages have belonged to the public, and those that were able to survive even in different format, such as the Latin language, are the languages, and the semantics of the public. Another evidence that can pinpoint the idea of history being common sense is in the construction of the meaning of the word common sense. The word "common" means intersection, shared by a number in the group. Meanwhile sense evolves a semantic content, a perception by means of using the senses and assigning indications to the surroundings. Hence common sense would come to mean an ordinary good sense and judgment. Among concepts within, theology, astrology and evolution theory, those that enjoy a good sense remain. Capitalism calls for the free market, indicating that the good ideas and practices would normally float and prevail. Theology announces the survival of the good in many probes, such as Noah's arch. Astrology proved that earth is the stage for common sense as well since there was no other inhabitant in our solar system. Meanwhile evolution theory indicates that survival is for the fittest, so far the fittest has been human and it is due to common sense, intelligence and judgments.

How can we create common sense from an ideological perspective? The construct I am about to propose beholds two cultures: the American culture in general, and *Hezbollah* culture. In the following diagram I am going to suggest an intersection between both societies. The intersection was due to common stimuli, that of a threat and danger to personal/ public space.

Both the American culture and the *Hezbollah* have a common stimulus. The stimulus is war. *Hezbollah* witnessed war with Israel concerning South Lebanon borders and a civil war; meanwhile American people have witnessed September 11 attacks, and war on Iraq. Although there is a direct and indirect influence for instance, war in Lebanon was a direct experience, whereas concerning the USA war was in an indirect manner, and partially away from the homeland.

After this initial stimulus, there have been changes in strategies, on different levels. These were social, emotional, economic, military and moral. All these factors led to a creation of communion within the society towards the threat. And they were experienced on several levels, in Lebanon, and the USA.

However, communion can be ideologically shared when the cultures are facing similar threats to their existence, such as invasion of space. Hence, empathy would create a motive towards the ideological common sense formation. Once this is formed, seeking peace is the first demand after war. Further, peace would develop into organizing experience for common good, such as an economical, intellectual, and social exchange. Thus, the intersection has evolved an ideological common sense.

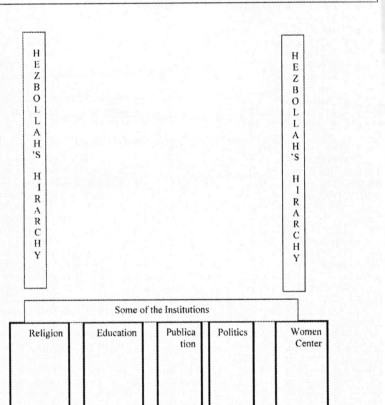

Affiliates/friends/strategies/history/religion/people

H E Z B O L L A H 'S H I R A R C H Y		H E Z B O L L A H 'S H I R A R C H Y

Some of the Institutions

Religion	Education	Publication	Politics	Women Center

The Population is mainly the majority of *Shia'a* from South Lebanon and Beqa'a Valley

Chapter IV
Symbolic Constructions of
Leadership in *Hezbollah*

Through the following chapter, subjects such as leadership constructs and charismatic characteristics are described and analyzed. Moreover, traditional Arab narratives where tales from 1001 Nights, parables from the Quran, and Shia'a Muslim History will present a unique cultural context for Hezbollah discourse. This chapter answers the question of the various symbolic constructions of leadership.

"*Abdullah*" the worshipper of God takes a new meaning in symbolic constructions of leadership within Hezbollah. Leadership has passed through various stages in the short history of the Islamic Resistance. Jihad, among other factors played an important role in these transitions. "*Abdullah*" is supposed to symbolize all means of worship, spiritual and material. We are all *Abdullah*s in the eyes of God; the Holy *Quran* states: "I only created the human and the jinni to worship". The concept of sacrifice (material and spiritual) is crucial in the definition of leadership. Above all God is the ultimate leader. He shall guide to the right path, and He does through the prophets, yet there is a process of selection in guidance; "And God shall guide whomever He pleases" the Holy *The Quran* states. Hence, if by innate behavior as discussed above we are all worshippers, yet on the other hand only selected people are guided, then the concept of *"Abdullah"* is at some point altered to fit a hierarchy system, which forms a continuum from extreme worship to non-believers.

The following narratives indicate how *Hezbollah* functions, which is through its leadership characteristics that were as well the product of various cultural themes.

Leadership and Charisma

Martyrdom played an important role in the formation of a strong, dedicated leader through the history of *Hezbollah*. Especially when *Nasrallah* offered his son as a martyr, and thus evening out himself the Secretary General with the rest of the resistance public, and thus transforming the collective consensus he is trying to convince people of to an individualistic one, while returning it back to being a collective belief. In order for a scholar to examine issues of leadership and charisma, one must make a quick review of the characteristics of leadership; furthermore, examine them within these rhetorical moments. Among the characteristics of leadership, Fairhurst (2001) cites Weber's argument of a charismatic leader, stating the sociohistorical context:

"Difficult times were fertile grounds for the emergence of charisma.-

-Charismatic authority was a potential revolutionary force and bridge between traditional and rational-legal forms of authority.

-Charismatic authority was naturally unstable, an instability that could produce one of two outcomes for charismatic social movements and the development of charisma (Weber, 1925/1968). Charisma either dies out in the departure of the leader from the social scene or becomes institutionalized and incorporated into the routines of everyday life" (p. 405).

It is evident that *Nasrallah* displays a great leadership qualities. These qualities bring him close to the public (Shia'a and non Shia'a), and bring the public close to him. He is the down to earth man, where triumph and victory were the significant characteristics of his ruling era. After the "open war" he was considered the leader who broke the Israeli army strength myth. *Nasrallah*, as his name indicates (the victory of God) was able to liberate South Lebanon, and regain the occupied territories. Bazi (2004) states when discussing *Nasrallah*'s charismatic character; "*Nasrallah* never envisioned to become a Secretary General, and he did not plan to be famous, where he enjoys the love of the public without any competition, those who know *Nasrallah* in the past, also know how careful he is to stay away from the lights, regardless of his known humble character, and eye catching shyness. Likewise, he is very faithful in his work to the extent of complete indulgence in his career, moreover, we cannot deny his bravery, strength when it comes to calling for the right" (p. 11).

The sociohistorical ground was paved for *Nasrallah* to walk smoothly towards the charismatic leadership. South Lebanon was under the Israeli occupation, "*Shia'a* Muslims were under tremendous pressure and marginalization, the former Secretary General was assassinated by the Israeli planes, and *Hezbollah* needed a successor who would proceed with the establishment and who was well aware with the organizational procedures. These factors among others, where able to institute *Nasrallah* in leadership, and his speech, as Bazi (2004) states, took three dimensions:

1. "An ideology that calls for an upheaval and renascence" (p. 13). *Nasrallah* calls the people not to be afraid, but to resist, not to subject to the status quos, but to work for development, not to fear the enemy, but to frighten it. On the other hand, *Nasrallah* calls not to indulge in self success, but to always be humble when attaining it whether individually or collectively.

Bazi (2004) quotes *Nasrallah's* speech *Victory Celebration*, given on May 26, 2000 in the liberated city of Beint Joubailin, Lebanon: "we are a nation that does not fall when faced by grief, nor do we fall when enjoying happiness" (p. 78). Bazi says, that *Nasrallah* was not the inventor of such balanced method, but these words are taken from the *Quran*, This methodology was taken from the *Quran*, "so you won't grief what passed you by, nor by that what struck you, and God knows all your deeds" (Al Omran, verse 135). "Don't be happy with what has been granted, for God does not like those who show off, and walk aimlessly"(Iron, verse 23).

2. "Human as a point of reference and the role of religion" (Bazi, 2004, p. 13). *Nasrallah* uses the human as the subject matter, he states that God appreciated human beings and made them superior to all other creations, hence the concepts of the party will function similarly. In his speech during the exchange of hostages and martyrs with Israel, Bazi reads *Nasrallah* quoting: "This accomplishment that makes us all proud, belongs to our civilization, religion, and culture, we are the nation that believes

in the freedom of human beings and his rights, human beholds respect when alive, and respect when dead, for human are the best in creation" (p. 13). According to the implication of the content, in other words, *Nasrallah* is calling for the democratic rule known in the West. He is as well showing a collective cultural behavior, when sharing the victory with the rest of the public. Although this quality is highly appreciated, but it is worth mentioning that indeed it is a quality of a superior leadership, as well as it might serve in increasing the popularity and decreasing the distance between the public and the leader. As an extension of U.S. President Kennedy's famous saying "ask not what your country can do for you, but what you can do for your country", *Nasrallah* is saying, this is what you have done for your country, and soon your country will pay you back your offering in security and other benefits, all this is accounted to be the outcome of resistance.

In other words, Bazi (2004) exclaims, "*Nasrallah* relates this accomplishment with the nation, all of the nation, not with the individual the party or a side, connecting the nation with religion" (p.13). When the Druse parliament member Walid Jumblat asked Nasrallah through a televised interview done with Future TV "who is he going to present this victory for?" meaning the victory to be accomplished after the "open war of July 2006, Nasrallah answered through another televised interview with Almanar TV, "It is to all of Lebanon".. Moreover, Fairhurst (2001) explains "One of the strongest oppositions in the charisma literature is that between the individual and the system. This opposition first surfaced in a non antagonistic pull away from the individual toward the relational, only to be followed by an antagonistic reframing in the reframing of the individual and the relational as too micro in factor and macro social system concerns" (p. 404).

3. "Mister Moussa Alsader is the leader of the Islamic Resistance" (Bazi 2004, p. 13). The third factor argued by Weber of a charismatic leader, takes a different leap here. *Nasrallah* derives the qualities of a great (missing) leader, who enjoyed a high status of respect among the public. *Nasrallah* gains credibility from the great leader of the Islamic Resistance, aided by an image transference from *Alsader*, the great *"Shia'a"* leader, his qualities, beliefs, and visions. Bazi (2004) states, "in conclusion, *Nasrallah* is no longer the educated revolutionary leader, and the good speaker that beholds his audience, all of his audience, and grasps the attention of all observers, but I think that Mister *Nasrallah* has become a thinker, a lecturer and aware of the struggle, and aware of his century's demands and nation's needs, in a struggle that is expected to last long" (p. 13).

Indeed there was an alteration in the character of the charismatic leader. A gradual shift that walked along the transformation that the *Party of God* underwent due to the social, political, and various contextual transformation the area was witnessing. That development is in all aspects a healthy progression, but on some of its corners a demand for survival, and in its others a mere requirement of life.

In two of the photos, that in which portrays *Nasrallah* and is supposed to be a sticker for the car or the window glass, the shift in appearance is evident. *Nasrallah*, in the first photo that dates to the late 1990s, he is a young leader, with a strong willing gaze, covered by black glasses, a fearless laugh, and a dark black beard and moustache, the background of that photo is *Hezbollah*'s yellow flag only. While in another photo, that dates to the years after the liberation of South Lebanon, *Nasrallah* has a calmer gaze, one that is comforting, a gaze that is covered by a thinner frame of his glasses, he looks older because of the white hair covering his beard, some of his hair and moustache, while this older look grants him a wiser appeal, meanwhile, the background of that photo is *Hezbollah*'s yellow flag adjacent to that of the Lebanese one. Hence, through appearance and through performance, *Nasrallah* portrayed a change in attitude.

For every leader, there is another leader that he/she aspires to. Bazi (2004) states about *Nasrallah*'s childhood, "*Nasrallah* was fascinated by the image of Imam Moussa Alsader. He was not like any of his peers, his friends would go out playing soccer, or swimming in the river, meanwhile he would go to the mosque in Sin Alfeel district, or Bourj Hammoud area, or the *Naba'a,* for there was no mosque in his area" (p. 18). Although the image of a worshipper, a dedicated believer is important in making of leadership qualities especially that of a Muslim one, however, within an organizational setting in which the *Party of God* has became, it is not sufficient. The preceding characters as much as they enhance *Nasrallah*'s educated Muslim image also harm it, for group work is essential in organizations, prayers alone are not sufficient to develop a leader, and leaving your friends for isolation decreases the skills in team work. It is widely known that many organizations, in job interviews, look for extra curricular activities in employees as evidence to their group work commitments. Swimming and playing soccer develop the personality of the individual. Prophet Mohammad said "teach your children archery, swimming and horse riding ", this saying not only to prepare them for war, or to make them physically fit, (where you can notice that *Nasrallah* enjoys a good health maybe some overweight, if comparing his height to weight) but also to promote group work.

Away from appearance, and still in the discussion of social affiliation, *Nasrallah* did not first appear with *Hezbollah*, on the contrary, he started off with Amal Group, "*Nasrallah* and his brother Hussein became members in Amal's party, where he was able to be the representative of his own village, regardless of his young age. His first political stop he went to Iraq to study then was forced to depart as many students, by the Iraqi forces and authorities back then" (p. 19). *Nasrallah*'s young age was not an impediment in a culture that associates wisdom with old age. Actually he was one of the first leaders that took power at a very young age, and still is (around 45 years old now); maybe his young age was a need for the *Party of God* at that time. They needed the strength of a man in his thirty's rather than the wisdom of the fifty's age. *Hezbollah* was passing through a difficult time at that point, strict reform was the main concern, and only a rebellious, strong, thirty-some-years-old leader with a vision could establish that mission. Wisdom, was a second concern, however, *Nasrallah*, showed a combination of both. Significantly, collectivism in decision making and public contribution are the fuel of charismatic leadership as argued and applied earlier, however, Fairhurst (2001) adds that "but Weber was also ambiguous and somewhat contradictory about the relative emphasis of the individual over the relational; while writing about the extraordinary qualities of charismatic leaders, he also repeatedly stressed that constituent's collective beliefs in the wisdom and knowledge of the charismatic was the crucial test of charisma" (p. 404).

A leader projects a vision, a vision for the future of the

public behind his/her popularity. Bazi (2004) states quoting *Nasrallah* " we have to admit that our party is bigger than the sect it belongs to (*Shia'a*) it is even bigger than any sect, it is bigger from any political scheme currently. We are a nation's wide project; our aims do not end at the Lebanese-Palestine borders. Disarming our forces does not get along with our ambitions and intellect, our size and glory, and the wide public support backing us. All this does not match to leave our weapons in order to gain a political stance such as a ministry chair, or to increase our members in the Lebanese parliament, in order to be enclosed within the local political games" (p. 35).

Nasrallah as a word, or event, or significant behavior was mentioned in the *Quran*. One of the Suras which is titled as "Victory" states, "When comes the victory of God (*Nasrallah*) and expansion, and thou dost see, the people enter God's religion in crowds, celebrate the praises of thy Lord, and pray for his forgiveness, for He is oft-Returning (in Grace and Mercy)] (Victory: 1-3). In other words, the Quran not only is mentioning Nasrallah in name, but also is promising that there is a day when the believers will rejoice and they will embrace the Islamic religion.

In another verse *Nasrallah* is mentioned in the *Quran*; "They encountered suffering and adversity. And were so shaken in spirit that even the apostle and those of faith who were with him cried "when will come the victory of God? Ah! Verily the help of God is always near!" (Albaqara: 214). In the awaiting of the victory of God, *Hezbollah* assigned a young leader, provoking victory and spelling its ground, *Nasrallah*, [the victory of God]. Such victory was attained through the liberation of South Lebanon. However the major belief is that God is the one whom beholds the chair, the chair of command. The *Quran* states "nor shall they compass aught of his knowledge except as he willeth his throne doth extend over the heavens and the earth, and He feelth no fatigue in guarding and preserving them, for He is the most High, the Supreme in glory" (Albaqara: 255). After all the command is that of God, and it is portrayed by the words present in the *The Quran*. This verse is also called the "Alkoursi" or the chair. The word Alkoursi is taken from the French Kater est isse, meaning sit on four legged chairs. Such indication proves the flexibility of language, and it symbolic significance.

Communication and language have always been a concern of the charisma and vision literature of the leader. The style of presenting, performance, word choice, irony, etc. envisions a leader. Political leader's style and vision in public communication settings, and the largely unacknowledged role that the media play in enhancing a charismatic persona are all subjects of study. Cognitive outcomes associated with the delivery aspects of a charismatic's style such as eye contact, fluid rate, gestures, facial expressiveness, energy, eloquence, and voice tone variety are all in tact here. For instance, *Nasrallah* has established two significant delivery styles; he mixes formal with informal expressions, thus varying his style from rigid and firm Arabic expressions to the informal, relaxed sentences that are familiar with the audiences' ears and cognitions. *Nasrallah* also poses between his sentences, and coordinates his silences, speech speed, hands movement, eye contact, tune level, organizing his black cap on his head, or even cleaning his sweat!

Fairhurst (2001) argues that "visions establish, maintain, or help cultures survive environmental fluctuations. They may also be the source of conflict and poor performance when discrepancies arise between the vision and some aspect of the environment" (p. 404). In the celebration of victory and liberation Bazi quotes *Nasrallah*'s speech; "the standards for victory was in the exchange of culture, there is a basic moral point in particular, this is the weapons that we revitalize it, by returning its audio and visual back to the minds and hearts in these days were many people were broadcasting negative themes, depressing titles, and bringing down the morals of people. This strategy is not new to the people, you have lived through it for more then twenty years, the standard rule of victory was that those who are passionate about death have defeated those who fear it, and those who see in death and martyrdom a path towards immortal life, defeated those who see in death as a stray way and mortality" (p. 88).

Jihad has been one of the most important stops through the *Party of God* leadership, and reorder. In order to light up heroism, there has to be a dark villain. Israel did not waste time in playing that role through the occupation of the land and the parallelization of the South Lebanon's, and other area's economy as well as various aspects of life, topped with the social security issue. Bazi quotes one of the questions asked to *Nasrallah*: "How were you able to convince someone to go eyes wide open to face death?"

Nasrallah answers, "thank God that among our forces there are people who hold their faith in God, His Heaven, and Judgment Day, for it wasn't for that faith, we would not be able to recruit anyone to face the toughest army in the area. These people who believe in God, Heaven, and the Day of Judgment, they come from every deep valley and they rush, no they compete to serve. If it weren't for this all, Islamic Resistance would not be able to develop and continue, and get closer to victory if God allows" (p.37). That strategy of good and bad is also evident in the American war over terrorism. When the national security is in danger, and interests are at stake, religion serves to unite people. Such an act has been proven through generations of military service and war. Whenever such threats surface, the leaders and planners automatically turn to something that brings people together, here Islam, Shia'ism and above all a One God serves the purpose.

Traditional Arab Narratives

The attitude towards sacrifice varies from the expected response towards tragedies of death. For instance, when *Nasrallah*, the present Secretary General of the *Party of God*, offered his son as a soldier, and later on a martyr, he did not accept condolences from people, on the contrary, he was asking people to come and rejoice with him because his son was able to join the rest of his friends in Heaven. Indeed, this active response reminds me of a story from "One Thousand and One Night", where it speaks of a fisherman, *Abdullah* the Land, fishes a merman, *Abdullah* the Sea. The two *Abdullah*s (or worshippers of God) make an arrangement to exchange gifts and cultural themes. *Abdullah* the Sea would bring out jewels and pearls from his exhibition, while *Abdullah* the Land, would bring out fruits, vegetables and other ornaments not found in the sea. A simple highlight of primitive commerce. However, the theme of the story climaxes when *Abdullah* the Sea invites that of the Land for a visit, where intercultural communication evolves. In order to make the trip possible, *Abdullah* the sea offers to cover *Abdullah* the Land's body with the a whale's oil (this might be another reference to the significance of whales that is similar to the story of the Prophet Jonah (*Younes*) who also used the whale for survival under the seawater when he was voted off the ship.

Abdullah the Land answers the invitation. Once in the water, the human passes through various strange habits and rituals, as well as amazing architecture. As he explores the different cultural rites, he passes by a group of people who are rejoicing, so he asks the merman:

Abdullah the Land: "Why are they so happy? Are they celebrating a wedding?"

Abdullah the Sea: "No, they are celebrating a funeral!"

Abdullah the Sea further explains that they rejoice because the person has returned to the Creator, and he questions the behavior in *Abdullah* the Land 's culture upon death, where the latter answers that they mourn and cry. The merman gets upset, and tells him that he does not like such behavior explaining that how could people mourn and cry if God retains what He has bestowed, such as life.

The main significance behind such intercultural dialogue is a symbolism pointing out to a discourse that might take place, at the present time, between the West and the East on a macro scale. In abstract, most cultures mourn for the departed and upon death. However, in concept, some as that of *Hezbollah*'s culture would not, especially when it comes to martyrdom. Upon the death of the martyr Hadi Hassan *Nasrallah*, the father or the Secretary General of *Hezbollah*, called on the people not to mourn, but to come and congratulate him, because his son has joined many of his friends in the heavens where they (martyrs) hold a high status.

When *Nasrallah* received the corpse of his son 's body through an exchange deal with Israel with a German mediatory, Bazi (2004) quotes the father 's reaction:

"I wanted to take a handkerchief from the table, to wipe my sweat, at least off my glasses, but I thought that among these television stations, that are broadcasting the ceremony to various foreign countries, some of which would sell their productions to Israel, hence people will assume that I am wiping my tears not sweat, I froze my hand and preferred to drawn in my sweat than to give the enemy the image of a distressed father, crying his eldest son, while calling the people to martyrdom" (p. 51).

The Afterlife

The belief in the after-life is one of the compensations for the Jihad. The whole concept is depending on it, and the true believer, the *"Moujahedeen"* are dependent on it. The concept is similar to the kamikaze's fighter in World War II. It is not the same, but at some point it has a common ground, that of securing a ground, or land. However, to a Western mentality, the concept of Jihad is made clear by recounting a myth, a one that is similar to the behavior of the *Party of God* upon military Jihad and martyrdom is that discussed by the anthropologist Paul Radin, in the Myth and Cosmos (1967). Such a myth will move the argument towards the construction of hierarchy within *Hezbollah*. The title of the myth is the "Two friends who became reincarnated: The origin of the four night's wake". This is the story of two friends, one of them is a chief's son, who decides to sacrifice their lives for the welfare of the community. After undergoing a series of ordeals in the underworld, they reach the lodge of earth maker, who permits them to become reincarnated and to resume their previous lives with relatives and friends (p.16). Because they died without responsibility of their own, but instead that of others, those will inherit the unspent part of their lives, while the heroes themselves will be permitted to return to earth and the same process will be repeated all over again (p. 17).

To sum up the meaning of the myth so far, Middleton (1967)

explains, if one wants a full life one gets a full death, if one renounces life and seeks death, then one increases the full life of his fellow-tribesmen, and moreover, secures oneself a state composed of an indefinite series of half-lives and half deaths. Thus we have a triangular system (p. 18).

Meanwhile, in one of his speeches (2002), *Nasrallah*, the secretary general of *Hezbollah* explains that the martyrs are gifted the highest ranks in Heaven. He adds that in the after life, God asks the martyrs and believers, whether they want to come back to life, most believers after seeing Heaven and enjoying its peacefulness, disregard the idea and prefer to stay in Heaven, only the martyrs, they request to come back to earth. *Nasrallah* adds, "They chose to do so because they want to fight again, for the sake of justice and because they know what high rank martyrs hold in Heaven".

Since hierarchy, as well as defense, is present in the after life, and it is referenced in the *Quran*; "We have lifted people in degrees above each other". While it is practiced in the animal kingdom (such as a bee soldier that would sacrifice its life when stinging for defense of the comb), and human social life across the centuries, as well as embedded within *Hezbollah*'s organizational constructs. In that construct, *Hezbollah* elected a council, Kassem (2004) states that;

> *"the first such elected council—which was the fourth in sequence—elected Sheikh Subhi al-Tufaili as Secretary General on November 11, 1989. A six month extension to this Council's term was granted given the impossibility of holding the annual Party conference (hostility between Amal and Hezbollah at the time had forced a siege on the Iqlim al-Tuffah area where the conference was to be held)"* (p. 63).

Since policies are not fixed, Kassem (2004) explains: "Thereafter, some policy amendments were made. Yet another reduction in the number of Council members was decided, bringing the total brought down to seven, which was more in accordance with assigned responsibilities, and the Council's term was decided to be two years. The Deputy Secretary General position was also created. In May 1991, the Council elected as Secretary General al-Sayyed Abbas al-Moussawi, who was martyred on February 16, 1992. The Council then elected as successor al-Sayyed Hassan *Nasrallah*, who came to effectively assume its term activities" (p. 63). *Nasrallah* is still the Secretary General as of 2006. When Bazi (2004) quoted a question about the separation between the military victory (through the resistance) and investigating it politically to serve a political jump, *Nasrallah* answered that such big question cannot be answered except through "digging that belief and politically, and military based institution that derives its name from the *Quran*, and that beholds a complicated method through its public relations with other forces, countries, organizations, *Party's*, and political trends starting from the Lebanese government, passing through Syria, and ending in the Islamic Republic of Iran, before heading towards the enemies and rivals, that chased and still chasing the Party under the accusation of terrorism" (p. 34). Hence under *Nasrallah*'s leadership Hezbollah experienced a period of transformation, reformation, and development.

Kassem (2004) states "the election of al-Sayyed Hassan *Nasrallah* occurred in Mid-May of 1993, and was to recur in the election rounds since then, inclusive of the seventh round of August 2003. Two amendments to the Council policies were passed over the period, the first of which was to extend its term to three years, while the second provided the Secretary General with the possibility of candidacy even following success in two consecutive elections" (P. 63).

Armory is the right and left arm of a leader/organization within any state. It is the security zone against various external threats. The *Party of God* was dependent on its military skill from the start. *Alkoudous Alarabi* in its issue published in 28/1/2004, and as cited by Bazi (2004), stated that "it is evident that in general the only language to communicate with Israel is that of which it uses to communicate with the rest of the world, and what is important politically and humanitarianly is that *Hezbollah* knew how to deal with this humanitarian case [hostages and martyrs exchange] all this time"(p. 452). Kassem, cited by Bazi (2004), ensures the power of weapon and implications of having hostages saying "we are not weak, we can accomplish a lot, on one condition that we should know what we need and to be ready to pay for the sacrifices in order to be liberated" (p. 21).

Kassem (2005) indicates the implications of Jihad. "Islam considers Jihad to be a basic behavior in a Muslim's life, be that a jihad with one's soul or a struggle against the enemy" (p. 36). Jihad is divided into two aspects: the military Jihad, and the Jihad with the soul. According to military Jihad, which is based on fighting the enemy, "religious clerics split military jihad into two parts, groundwork jihad, which is the confrontation of the Muslims with others and the entry into others" lands for reasons not tied to the reclamation of land or the fighting of aggression…defensive jihad, this is the defense of Muslims of their land, their people or their own selves upon facing aggression or occupation" (p. 39). The expectations of leadership are rooted long before our present time. A battle that has been going on since the Prophet Mohammad 's [PBUH] time period. Kassem (2005) states, "the prophet [PBUH] said that he who dies without conquest, and does not even speak to his soul of it, has died on a basis of falseness" (p. 43). Kassem continues citing Imam Ali (PBUH) saying "death shall defeat you in life, and you shall defeat life through death" (p. 43).

"Shiaism"

The word *"Shi'ah"* in the Arabic Dictionary *Almounjed* is the derivative of the word (Sha'a), meaning to spread. Nasr (2004) translating the Tabataba'i states that "Shia'ah which means literally party or follower, refers to those who consider the succession to the prophet upon whom be blessing and peace to be the special right of the family of the prophet and who in the field of the Islamic sciences and culture follow the school of the Household of the Prophet" (p. 47). However such definition does not fully satisfy the voracious social appetite of contemporary Islam. For in deed and practice, many Sunni do as well follow the school of the household of the Prophet, and the thirteen centuries or more of cold and hot wars among both sects has as well brought in vaccinations of implicit and explicit cultural exchanges.

Therefore, there is a great need to step down from definitions and semantics to the historical background of Shia'ism. Geertz (2001) indicates that the word definition comes from the Latin origin of *definitions* meaning to kill and make final. Here, I don't intend to make final, on the contrary I am working on making an introduction, to the sect's formation. Naser (2004) indicates that "Shi'ism began with a reference made for the first time to the party of Ali (Shi 'at Ali), the first leader of the Household of the Prophet, during the lifetime of the Prophet himself" (p. 49).

Meanwhile, the *Quran* itself referenced the word Shia'h, when in one of the verses it said "don't disintegrate into sects". Nevertheless, what concerns me here is beyond the dispute that this verse might provoke, is that Shi 'ism was even mentioned before the Prophet's designation of "Imam Ali" as his successor and inheritor, as Nasr references the Prophet's speech that "whoever would be the first to accept his invitation would become his successor and inheritor, Ali was the first to set forth and embrace Islam" (p.50).

Although both sects Sunni and Shi 'ite agree that Imam Ali, peace upon him, was preserved from error and sin in his actions, the separation between them both was inevitable. Most *Hezbollah* members belong to the Shi 'ite, maybe because the development of the sect was in South Lebanon where the majority of inhabitants are the Shi 'ite Muslims, yet special cases might exist, and it also emphasizes the multilayered nature of the sects in Lebanon.

When tackling the issue of leadership, in *Hezbollah* and Islam, I feel obliged to discuss Imam Ali, peace upon him, which is referenced to be a model for speech making and leadership. Imam Ali, was able to make to the *"Shia'a"* sect what I have called in this study, "commonsense". Belsey (1994) indicates that "common sense itself is ideologically and discursively constructed, rooted in a specific historical situation and operating in conjunction with a particular social formation" (p.3). To discuss Ali's leadership is to in some way review a past/present era in handing the torch among Muslims, especially *"Shia'a"*. Al-Jibouri (2002) narrates the story of succession:

"Ali was born in 600 A.D. inside the precincts of the Ka'ba, the holiest of holy places, where no other human being besides him was ever born. Muhammad was then thirty years old. Ali first opened his eyes on the sacred face of Mohammed who lovingly took him in his arms and gave him his first bath. That was a prediction that this same baby would give Mohammed his very last bath, his funeral bath, one's favor reciprocated by the other. For several days after his birth, Ali accepted no milk but the moisture Mohammed's tongue which he sucked and whereby he was nourished. Ali felt comfortable in Mohammad's lap and slept often by his side in the same bed, enjoying the warmth of his cousin's body and inhaling the sacred fragrance of his breath. When he grew up, Ali followed Mohammad like his shadow and on many occasions offered his life as a sacrifice for his own" (p.542).

Ya'qub (1999) states that the Islamic political system is that applied by the Prophet (PBUH) during his divine solicitation for organizing relations with his followers. As this solicitation was developed into a government, the Prophet applied the same system during his leadership which lasted for ten years (p. 106). Ya'qub, furthermore, explains the four pillars the Islamic political system is based upon. Concerning leadership, the first pillar discusses. Ya'qub states that "political leadership is a very divine doctrine, among which Islam, is nominated or elected directly by God. Applied to this fact are the prophets David, Solomon and Mohammed" (p. 106). Ya'qub, the author of *The Conception of the Sahaba's Ultimate Decency and the Political Authority in Islam*, explains that there are two ways in which God notifies his decision, directly and indirectly, "on the indirect notification of God's selection, is God's nominating *Ali-bn-Abi-Talib* as the successor of Mohammed, the leader of the nation. This preference had been wide spread declared by Mohammed in the sight and hearing of one hundred thousand Muslims. That was in the Prophet's last ritual pilgrimage, the Farwell Pilgrimage" (p. 107).

On the other hand, Kassem (2005) cites Imam Khomeini's saying about the jurist-theologian authority: "The illusion that the Prophet's leadership authority was higher than that of the commander of the Faithful, or that the latter's authority was higher then that of the Jurist Theologian, is but a delusion. It is doubtless that the Prophet's virtues are more numerous than those of all people, but the sum of the moral virtues does not increase one's ruling authority. Those same mandates awarded to the Prophet and the Imams (PBUH) in terms of mobilizing soldiers, assigning rulers and governors, collecting taxes and redistributing wealth among Muslims have also been provided by God Almighty to the governments of today. More than one person was chosen by God and assigned this authority. This assignment was rather bestowed on he who symbolizes knowledge and justice" (p. 53).

The struggle for power is not only a Western concern, nor is it merely an organizational one. It is rather a world-wide conception that has been battled through the ages. The battle for leadership has long been the concern of the two sectarian groups, Sunni and *Shia'a*. After discussing the indirect divine legitimacy of Imam Ali, Ya'qub (1999) states that "they [*Shia'a*] also allege that God has nominated Al-Hassan and Al-Hussein respectively as the successors of Imam Ali, and arranged this question in the form that every Imam should nominate his successor" (p. 210). However, there is still the conception of Sunnism, which means pursuing the Prophet's traditions. Yet, Ya'qub states "Unlike the belief adopted by the public, Sunni does not indicate pursuing the Prophet's traditions. Shia'a, in fact are the most careful for pursuing the Prophet's deeds, words, and signature" (p. 211). In order to further this claim, Ya'qub states two evidences: the individual authority, and the congregational authority. "The individual authority was held by the—foremost head of the Prophet's house hold; Ali (PBUH). This authority faces the predominant ruler's dictatorship for Sunnis" (p. 211). As for the congregational authority, it "was held by the Prophet's progeny and household. These individuals were loyal to their head. They sided him in conserving sturdy origins of the religion" (p. 212).

As mentioned in Chapter II that the name *Hezbollah* or the *Party of God* derives from the *Quran*. "Your friend can be only Allah, and His messenger and those who believe, who establish worship and pay the poor due, and bow down [in prayer]. And whosoever taketh Allah and His messenger and those who believe for friends [will know that], Lo! The party of Allah, they are the victorious" (Almaeda: 56).

Many interpretations of the Holy *Quran* remarked that the Holy Verse involved had been revealed for Ali. Ya'qub states that "these two verses were revealed for Ali when he gave his ring as alms while he was performing the ritual genuflection of the prayer" (p. 212). Furthermore, Ya'qub debates that "as he saw Ali give his ring as alms while he was in his ritual genuflection of the prayer, Mohammed, the Prophet (PBUH), recited the words Moses, the prophet, had supplicated his Lord with: (And give me an aider from my family, Ali. Strengthen my back by him...)" (p. 212).

Hence, there is a connection between leadership, past present, and the naming of the *Party of God*, while that of the

Sunni and *"Shia'a"* entrenched conflict for power, and leadership, internal and external. When referencing the verse, where the name of the *Party of God* was taken, according to *"Shia'a"* theologians, for instance, A-Qwasheji's Sharhul-Tajrid, and many others, we are as well referencing a verse that is related to Ali (PBUH) and in part is related to *Hezbollah.* When balancing up such equation, and away from the known fact that *Hezbollah* is a *"Shia'a"* sect, the outcome would evidently be that *Hezbollah* as well support Ali for Leadership of the Muslim nation.

The Story of Karbala

I choose to delve in the subject matter of Karbala's tragedy referencing a story written for children to emphasize the theme of leadership that many generations are brought up to through such rhetoric, and latter on rites and rituals such as these that are practiced in Nabatieh (the themes will be further discussed later on). In the following story, the battle could take the shape of descendants the prophet's blood [People of the House] later to be called the *"Shia'a"*, making of relativity theory, in social life the main theme here.

"Bird: Why are you crying, Moon?"

"Moon: Had you known what I know, you wouldn't have asked."

"Bird: And what is it that you Know, Moon?"

"Moon: What I know, Bird, would make a stone cry, because back then, it made everything on earth and in the sky cry; angels, humans, and animals. You were not there, but I was, and I saw everything. The desert, the stars, the sky, the trees, and the river were all there too, and they all saw how Imam Hussein (Peace be upon him) and his family and friends were killed extremely thirsty, even though the river was nearby". (p. 8)

"When Al-Zahraa grew up, she married Ali Bin Abi Taleb (P.), the Prophet's cousin. Ali (P.) was the best person after The Prophet (P.) He resembled him in his beliefs and in his behavior, especially that he was brought up in the Prophet's own house, and spent most of his time with him" (p. 11). Yazid wanted to kill Imam Hussein (PBUH). Imam Hussein wanted to go to the Kufa, the city where his father Imam Ali (PBUH.) had lived. In the Kufa, people were waiting for Imam Hussein to come so they wrote letters to him telling him how much they loved him, and asked him to come to the Kufa as fast as possible (p. 17).

"Some people were cowards and left Muslim and went home. Although they gave their word Imam Hussein, they didn't keep their promise because they were sacred of Yazid. Others left Imam because Yazid promised to give them money, land and other things is they disobeyed Imam Hussein and didn't fulfill his demands" (p. 24).

"Muslim: O Allah, be the judge between us and those people who have fooled and betrayed us. They asked us to help them, but they have given us to our enemy to kill us" (p. 30).

Ibn Sa'ad: We know that you are the son of the Prophet's (p.) daughter, and that you are an inerrant Imam. We don't want to kill you, but you must obey the orders of Yazid and accept his authority and induct him" (p. 55).

Imam Hussein (p.): No, By Allah! A man like me won't put his hand in the hands of the devil and his followers. I would never accept to oppress people by letting a tyrant like Yazid rule them. Yazid is an unjust and oppressive ruler that is known to be a drunkard and a killer of the holy souls.

Imam Hussein (p.): Woe unto you, Sufians. If you had no

religion, behave as Arabs and be free once in your life. It's me whom you are fighting, not the women and children. You have nothing to do with them as long as I 'm alive.

Sun: Shimmer replied telling him that he would have what he asked for. So, they came back to him. One of them approached the Imam and struck him with the sword on his head. The Imam said, "May you never have the ability to eat or drink with your right hand, and may Allah cram you with the unjust people in hell

They gathered against him, striking him till his body was full of wounds and bruises. He passed out at one time, and awoke at another. The enemies stood there confused, and his horse kept circling around him until it was stained with the Imam's blood" (p. 143).

The proceeding story shows how children are raised up on remembering the "case," namely, the tragedy of Imam Hussein in Karbala'a with all its violence and brutality. Such story serves as a recruitment strategy. It is a strategy of transference of a case, a battle against tyranny and hardship. The ultimate price paid here is the lives of some of the closest people to God. For the enemy it is saying that the Shia'a people are *"Karbala'i"* people. Meaning the tragedy forms an important role in their history, and since it does that for centuries there will be no stopping to their "case" regardless of time, till they achieve their curriculum! This tragedy is a role model to the children so they would realize the importance of sacrifice for the nation-state.

Recruiting Young Men

"Islam carries tremendous recruiting potential for its followers. Concentration on the spiritual aspects of life, abandonment of those bodily and spiritual pleasures in favor of the more virtuous goals, the promise of being a member of the *Party of God* and of the Almighty's blessing, all empower the Muslim in his quest for achieving true belief and defending his thesis" (Kassem 2004, p. 43).

Furthermore, the *Quran* has expressed these two aspects as the two rewarding attributes: "Say: can we wait for us aught save one of two good things [death or victory in Allah's way], while we await for you that Allah will afflict you with a doom from Him or at our hands. Await then! Lo! We are waiting with you" (*the Quran*, Al-Toubah, 52).

A society nurtured with the exemplary story of Imam al Hussein (PBUH) and his followers is enriched and reinforced by their conduct. Kassem (2004) states that since the meager number of devotees in the *Husseini* jihad was never an obstacle to Imam al Hussein (PBUH), and since the modest battle resources available did not deter them from going to battle, and since the choice that was limited to either victory or defeat, combat or martyrdom, was sealed in favor of martyrdom, what then could be possible justification for his nation's present day succumbing to oppression and submission to tyranny? (p. 45).

Members of the *Party of God* will explain their devotion to Jihad saying that "we have learned through Imam al-Hussein that the love of martyrdom is part of the love for God". Issues of Shiaism, parables of Imam Hussein and Karbala all are lessons that are being taught at schools, and throughout the various and diverse gatherings of Hezbollah. Kassem adds, "we have learned to glorify jihad for the sake of Islam. Generations after al-Hussein's resurgence in Karbala, we still learn from the magnificent accomplishments that materialized through his martyrdom. His vision was not momentary and restricted to the battle: it was directed at the future of Islam and Muslims (p. 45).

Whenever faced by any type of fear one of the responses in defense of Jihad will be as Kassem exclaims "all that the enemy is capable of is implanting the fear of death in us. When we halt this fear, we render the power of death with which he menaces us futile". In addition to it all is that we walk forward, reinforcing morale and marking gains on the path of victory, and we accumulate these positive achievements across time while waiting for the sought change to take place: Victory cometh only from Allah, the mighty, the wise (*the Quran*, Al-Imran, 126).

Leadership is ever continuous, it does not dry out, for the Christians, as well Muslims, and it is the Christ that would be resurrected again and come back to save the world. Meanwhile, for the *"Shia'a"*, there is an Imam al-Mahdi, al-Majlisi (2003) states that "on the authority of the Ghiyath Ibn Asad: The heir al-Mahdi, divine bliss be upon him, was born on Friday. His mother was a woman of dignity. She was called Narjis, Saqil, and Susan. She was called Saqil for the reason of the pregnancy. His birth was on the eighth night left from Sha'ban of the year two hundred and thirty six" (p. 32). Majlisi adds "she was called Saqil for the reason of the pregnancy, alludes to the illumination and glow that overtook her due to the luminous pregnancy. When they polish and shine their swords, Arabs call them Saqil" (p. 32).

The awaited Imam, has certain attributions, traits and lineage. Al-Majlisi (2003) states Musa Ibn Ja'far was cited saying "No one can be the Qa'im but an Imam the son of an Imam and a Successor the son of a Successor" (p. 70).

There are verses that state the rise of the Qa'im. Such verses are cited by al-majlisi (2003): Behold the day he comes to them. He is not turned aside from them and they will be encompassed by what they mocked (the Quran, Hud:8). Some people confuse between al-Mahdi and Jesus, however Al-Majsidi says "narrations from the apostles about the Mahdi are in inordinate numbers with multitudes of narrators, describing that he will rule for seven years and will fill the earth with justice, that Jesus the son of Mary will come with him and will assist him in killing the *Dajjal* (anti Christ) at the gate of Ladd in Palestine, that he will be the leader of this Ummah at that day and that Jesus will pray behind him, and all the other details of his enterprise (p. 160).

The proceeding was a reading of the symbolic constructions of leadership. I hope it might work to bring the shadowy images of the *Party of God* to substantial ones that are sensible and envisioned. Similar to Plato's cave here, within Plato's cave, what Plato was illustrating in the Myth of the Cave is the philosopher's road from shadowy images to the true ideas behind all natural phenomena. For I truly believe that there is an explanation for every phenomena, and to trace out the roots is not only an interesting phenomena but also an enlightening one. Plato's point was that the relationship between the darkness of the cave and the world beyond corresponds to the relationship between the forms of the natural world and the world of ideas. Here, thoughts are translated to words then action. A leader's word will form an upheaval, and the action would translate into Jihad, against tyranny. In sum, I recommend a study that looks at the social and economic status of Hezbollah members, as further step in the analysis of their rhetoric.

Chapter V
Organizational Reality and Language Codes

Arabic Language Codes

Lull (2000) states, "any one who speaks more than one language understands very well that language is much more than words" (p. 139). In other words, one cannot underestimate the power of language. Within it are embedded, various codes, cultural codes that are unique to each culture and very well practiced and well woven and braided in the behavior patterns, to the extent that we (as members of the culture) do not fully recognize their original meaning. A magical spell is not arbitrarily named a "spell". Language explains culture especially that of the Arabic culture, where the miracle of the *Quran* is strictly focused on the language issue. The curvilinear progression has always been a thought, a word and maybe an action. Arguing it, a word at some point could be merged with the action. Lull adds, "as the American anthropologist Michael Agar points out above, language is one surface of a deep and complex system of concepts we call culture. We cannot separate language from culture; they are intimately connected through meaning" (p. 139).

This chapter addresses the question of the organizational reality revealed through language codes. It will concentrate on language patterns, codes, and practices. Furthermore, it will discuss the relationship between language and performance.

As mentioned earlier, the Arabic culture is fused within language. For instance it is one of the cultures whose language and cultural name are the same. Arabic means literally "grammatical formation". For instance, Hassan and Hussein [PBUT] are the children of Imam Ali. Like the indigenous people, Native Americans in the USA, names hold meanings. The name Ali means high status. The name Hassan is derived from beauty. Hussein is the making of the name Hassan smaller (minimizing). Hence when *Nasrallah* says in one of his speeches in Karbal 'a, "I am part of Hussein, and Hussein is part of me" he is not only reminding the audience of the massacre that brutally murdered Hussein (through the discussion of incidents), but as well he is sublimely referencing the beauty within the name as well. The equation would sum up of course after mentioning that Hussein has a derivative of good deed "*hasana*" it will equal that I am relative of the "People of the House". His audience will understand that extension whether through beauty or through blood.

Elaboration and artistic exploration in the Arabic language are endless. A lion has more then ten identifications, more than ten name callings. In an open sea of words, and a culture that floats with wide expressions, it is evident that the miracle of Prophet Mohammed would be language. Language here does not only mean words, but as well numbers. The *Quran* states that it is a numerical book, which means that it is timely and well-measured. An exploration of language would as well mean an exploration of numbers which will soon be the subject matter of our discussions. Meanwhile, it is evident that numbers are the simplest languages. Lindloff (1995) adds; "not only is mathematics a precise and universal language, it represents quantities, relationships, and transformations in ways that seem to mirror nature itself" (p. 247-248).

On the other hand, the right one for most of us, where we use language codes to communicate, al-Jabouri (2002) states, "the Holy *Quran* was the evident miracle which sufficed all mankind as proof testifying to the truth of the message brought by Muhammad. Every syllable in it is a miracle by itself".

Language, by all means is important to the Muslim culture, al-Jabouri adds, "no human being can ever be acquainted with all the knowledge embedded in the Holy *The Quran*, for it is the speech of the Almighty, the Praised and Glorified One, Who has said, "[Say: If the sea were ink for the words of my lord, the sea would surely be consumed before the words of my Lord are exhausted even if We were to bring the like of it and add thereto]" (*The Quran*, 18:109). Meanwhile, Lull (2000) proclaims "though language maybe one surface of culture, personal interpretation and uses of language are by no means superficial, the most profound meanings are fashioned through language" (p. 139). In other words, we play with language, we ornament it, we ideologize it, and most certainly, it reflects us, our status, and capabilities. Lull explains "we learn who we are, and who they are, largely through language. Agar defines culture as something you make up to fill in the spaces between them and you. Language is about differences in the way people live" (p. 139). Thus language and culture within a society do walk hand by hand.

Now that it is evident that there is a great emphasis on

language in the Arabic culture, the *Quran* states "Seest thou not how God sets forth a parable? A goodly word, like a goodly tree, whose root is firmly fixed, and its benches (reach) to the heavens, it brings forth its fruit, at all times, by the leave of its Lord. So God sets forth parables for men, in order that they may receive admonition. And a parable of an evil word, is that of an evil tree, it is torn up by the root, from the surface of the earth, it has no stability" (Ibrahim: 24,26).

These verses emphasize the power of language, good language, and the consequences of the bad one. A format of communication, even when calling for non- Muslims to join Islam it is advocated to preach with the good wordings. A saying of the Prophet Muhammad says; "if thy were harsh in words, people would have disintegrate away from you". The *Quran* adds "God will establish in strength those who believe, with the Word that stands firm, in this world and in the hereafter" (Ibrahim: 27). Again, God through the *Quran* promises that the gratifications of the believers are in firm words. Thus words are at some level compared or even equivalent to actions. Although the Western philosophy, especially that set by Burke (1974) speaks of the sequence of thoughts, words than actions. The Arabic Muslim society goes deeper then the thoughts that are simply generated from input/ output of the society to discuss the intentions. The *Quran* mentions something similar to that saying that a person will earn whatever they have hidden in their intentions.

The Arabic language is complex in construction, an example of that is the "AlKoursay" verse. AlKoursay is a word meaning chair. The verse indicates that God almighty is all Knowing, all Compassing and nothing escapes His wisdom. The point behind this is that the name Alkoursy is derived from the French word *kater isse*, which means to sit on a four legged thing. Hence it proves that the wordings of the *The Quran* are indeed congressional and alternative with other languages.

To discuss the codes and language of *Hezbollah* it is of great importance to tackle the codes presented by the *Quran*. For the organization is not far from the manifestation of the Islamic religion. For instance, al-Jabouri says that "there are miracles in the Holy *Qur'an* which are continuous, perpetual, eternal, ever present, impressing one generation after another: each generation will by itself discover the miracles of this Book and may come to know that the miracles of the Holy Qur'an never end, nor will its wonders" (p. 704).

These words are not only al-Jabouri's thesis, for, Allah Almighty has said in the Holy *Quran*, "We will soon show them Our Signs in the universe and in their own selves till it becomes quite clear to them that it is the truth" (*The Quran*, 41:53). Its challenge, and the fact that it tears down the veil separating us from the future, is another difficult front which the enemies of Allah have to face [Indeed, I have experienced this fact of the *Quran*]. Al-Jabouri states that its knowledge of the future may be divided into two time periods: the first is the present and the near future, which is not distant from the time when the Holy *The Quran* was revealed, and the second is the distant future.

In the present, many Shia'a Muslims believe that history has been not fair to them. It burned, erased or did cover "their story". This at some point would explain *Hezbollah*'s determination and emphasis on having a recorded, saved rhetoric. To some people Imam Ali who centuries ago, spoke of generating electricity is quite vague, and this argument of course traces back to the history and its possibility of objective recordings. Tabatabai (2004) states, "in science and knowledge, Ali was the most learned of the companions of the

Prophet and of Muslims in general. In his learned discourses, he was the first in Islam to open the door for logical demonstration and proof and to discuss the divine sciences or metaphysics (*ma'arif Ilahiyah*)" (p. 217). Tabatabai adds that Ali (PBUH) spoke concerning the esoteric aspect of the *Quran* and devised Arabic grammar in order to preserve the *Quran's* form of expression. However, if one ever to speak of language, literally expressions, etc. Imam Ali is the person to be referenced most in the *"Shia'a"* Islam, for his fluency and sublime explanations of the world.

Going back to the *Quran*, the following are arguments that prove the timeliness of the Quran and its ability to predict near and far future. Let us deal with time/space theory in a physical manner, or the present, and near future stages in a little more detail. Concerning that of the Present and the Near Future the holy *The Quran* states:

[Aleef, Lam, Meem. The Romans have been vanquished, in a near land, and they, after being vanquished, shall be the vanquishers, within a few years. Allah's is the command before and after, and on that day the believers shall rejoice, with the help of Allah; He helps whomsoever He pleases, and He is the Mighty, the Merciful] (*The Quran*, 30:1-5).

AL-Jabouri questions, could Prophet Mohammed predict the result of a war that would be waged between two giant nations of that period of time, namely the Romans and the Persians, after a few years, and can the leader predict the fate of a war and guarantee the victory of one army over another (p. 705). This he says is a miracle; however, if one ponders in the timeless language of the *Quran*, he/she would not only limit the verse to a victorious war of one nation over the other. I would start to interpret such verse by segmenting references, such as the word "Romans" it is not only the reference of the past civilization. There are various meanings to the word "Rome" other then that of a culture. Rome is a derivative of the word "Rama", which means to want something, or to accomplish one thing after another in progression, when defined *alram* would mean a swamp. Hence the reference here would not only envelop the Roman people, but it will also exceed it to all those who would want something. But isn't that the case of all human? Here comes the intention at play. To want something is a human nature, what to want is a human will. And intention of victory or defeat is rather adjacent to good or bad will. Another example is the word Britain, El-Koussa (2001) references that "it is said that the name Britain comes from Prutani, a name given to the celts by the Romans. We, however believe that the Phoenicians gave the name *"Bar-Tanak"* which means the "the Land of Tin" to Britain which was their secret reservoir of tin, hence they used to bring it home or commerce with it" (p. 36). Keeping in mind that according to some Hezbollah rhetoric, this prediction is continuous, Italy or Rome did play an important role in the recent war of July 2006, it hosted a conference where the UN, the Foreign Minister of the USA, and Lebanese Prime Minister attended and a seize fire failed to take place. In addition to that, Italy won the European football World Championship!

The naming whether cultural or geographical and even material can definitely lead to the sublime symbolism of our world. It can form a guide, "daleel" in Arabic, which is partially the derivative of the Aramaic. Delilah, the mistress of Samson is again a reference that she was the woman to guide the Jews to Samson's point of power, and what was more eloquent in the story of Samson and Delilah, is that it is still existing now, between the Palestinians and the Israelis, and the power of Samson, which was in his hair, is only another symbol towards the power of language. Hair, in Arabic means Sha'ar, which is a derivative of the word sha'ara, which is feelings. And Samson's power was embedded within his feelings, once Delilah was able to grasp it, she locked Samson in the cell of love, and later on prison. Contradictory to what most scientists believe, the hair is not dead cells, it is rather like a silk of transmission from the outer perceptive vibrations of the world, towards the inner ones. And when Samson's hair grew back, and he regained his power, the famous saying "let it fall over me and my enemies", and he destroyed the temple over himself and the people within, is still in tact in the Israel/Palestine, where martyr's are almost everyday exploding themselves, and maybe having that saying deep within.

It is definite from previous arguments that relationship between *Hezbollah* and the *Quran*, hence language, social structure and framework are under the Book's codes of conduct. The *Quran* is not only social rules and political system. It is as well as said before a language miracle, a communication one, that between the Holy, the Divine, the One, and the Worshippers.

The miracles of time, as played in language in *Quran* are endless; after all it is a communication of a world, universe, with its physicality and metaphysicality. Of these challenges are some in which the world is partially fighting over, transportation. This fiery challenge "which puts an end to any confusion, forcing the unbelievers to recognize the fact that there is no doubt in this speech, the speech of Allah, the One and only God, and that it is capable of facing the unknown regarding the past, the present, and the future. This additional challenge is embedded in the verses saying;

"You will most certainly ride a stratum (of sphere) over a stratum". (*The Quran*, 84:19).

This statement was made more than one thousand and four hundred and fifty years ago when there were no planes, rockets, spaceships, not attempts to probe the earth 's outer sphere, and when means of transportation were confined to riding the backs of animals" (al-Jabouri 2002, p. 706).The author goes on explaining that the Almighty and the praised One promised the humans that they would ride one stratum of sphere after stratum, that is that they would be able to transverse the universe and move from one spherical orbit to another (p. 707).

Moreover, it is quite evident the emphasis on language in the *Quran*, and later one the reflection of such language on the *Party of God* codes of conduct and speech, if not in action then it is in call. As mentioned earlier that numbers formulate a language of their own. Such language was established years and years ago, and the wonder to its significance is still symbolic and many times altered. For instance, El-Koussa (2001) in his book, Pythagoras: the Mathmagician introduces what the Phoenician-Greek philosopher discussed about the numerical language. One of the topics I agree with is the definition of one as being the representation of the God, the unification of the whole creation. I will have another in the numerical poetics sometime soon. However, the numerical miracle of the *Quran*, al-Jabouri presents a first handy elaboration stating that the year, for example, is comprised of 365 days; therefore, the word "yawm", meaning day, is repeated exactly 365 times, while the word "shahr", meaning month, is repeated twelve times, and the word "sa 'a", meaning hour, is repeated twenty four times, signifying the total number of hours in the day (p. 714).

The Christians and Jewish believe that the whole world started with a word "At the start there was the word of thy Lord, Be to the universe, and the universe was created". That word of creation, "the be" was continuous along other religions such as Islam, and indeed if creation started with the verb to be, then it sure did end along the same methodology, of words, and the miracle of the *Quran* came to be in wordings. On that track, you would find that Islam was so much involved in the creation, coding and decoding of language. If Islam was involved in such language usage, so was the *Party of God*. Almanar television, Albasha 'ar radio station, speeches of *Nasrallah* published both through audio-visual stations or/and through print word. Speeches of the politicians involved with the *Party of God*, and various other publications and wordings (leaflets, billboards, newspapers, etc.) that form what I would call the new rhetoric of *Hezbollah*, not only that, but also a Research Center for documentation and historization of such rhetoric was developed.

Rhetorical Criticism of Publications

The following is a list of books that Hezbollah published. From the metanalysis of the titles, such strategy will give an idea of the topics and lines of thoughts. The Consultative Center for Studies and Documentation leaflet contains the following books. It should be regarded that the list is mainly concerned with economic issues developing in Lebanon, along with it is the political situation in Lebanon, which as well is sensitive to *Hezbollah*, and to the economic situation in Lebanon:

1. The Socio Economic Crises in Lebanon: Towards a comprehensive strategy for alternative policies.

The book includes papers and discussions of the economic conference held in Beirut on 12-13 Feb. 1999. This book contains the papers and discussions of this conference which shed light on the Crisis (the socio economic one, that Lebanon has been facing): Its various reasons, its aspects, and how it influences the Lebanese people in their daily life. In addition, what kind of procedures should the government take in order to ameliorate the economic situation? This book offers important ideas as for reformation.

2. The organization of the Local authorities in Lebanon: Towards a comprehensive application of the decentralized-system.

A study panel, conducted in the year 1999. This book is the fruit of the team-work discussion, and a panel, held on 27 August 1999, experts and well experienced representatives of Hezbollah in enriching this study and pin-pointing the useful way of implementing decentralization in Lebanon, which may facilitate and respond to citizens needs.

3. The Proportional Representative System in Lebanon.

This book contains a number of papers concerning the application of the proportional, representative system in Lebanon. Hezbollah representatives through their profound attempts, try to answer some problematic issues regarding the elective system. In their panel, held in 1999, organized by the center. The experts opened the endless discussion about the technical difficulties which confront the representation of the religious sects in various Lebanese provinces.

4. The Clash of Civilizations

Huntington's thesis of The Clash of Civilizations, created another clash disputes and global criticisms from eminent academicians in human sciences. This book contains critical responses to Huntington's thesis from Arab and non-Arab experts. It also includes interviews with Huntington.

5. The Lebanese Economy against the GAT Treaty

This book tries to unveil the ambiguity concerning the

Lebanese economy against the GAT treaty. It includes the main goals, principles and some modifications of the treaty. What would be the consequences of this treaty on Lebanon? This question is what the book tries to answer.

6. In Bringing about a Harmonized Law and Fortify Impartiality, When Handling Public Policies.

Four problematic issues are raised in this book:

1. The proportional electoral law.
2. Decentralization of the administration
3. The separation between the posts of the parliament and the ministry.

Answers to these issues assist in bringing about a harmonized law and fortifying impartiality, when handling public policies.

7. The Power-range of the Political *Parties* in South Lebanon

This book is an unprecedented study regarding the electoral operation in Lebanon. It establishes a pattern of analysis based especially on statistical methodology. It includes a detailed estimation of the power-range of the political *Parties* in South Lebanon mainly the southern province.

8. Alisar: Now and the Forthcoming Changes

Alisar is on the western-edge of the Beirut suburbs. This study is based on papers presented at a panel.

9. The Eighth War

This book documents the events that occurred during the eight war in South Lebanon. The Israeli criminal aggression in April 1996. It is a daily document that records 16 days of battles wherein the Islamic Resistance and the Lebanese people achieved their victory against the Israeli advanced military machine.

10. Ansariya, a Symbol for Victory

In an open war against the Israeli enemy, nine chapters

constitute an epic written by the strugglers for freedom. Know everything about the battle of Ansaryiyya where the Israeli mythical army was dispersed.

Mission of the Consultative Center for Studies and Documentation:

The Center (C.C.S.D) is a specialized scientific institute in Beirut, Lebanon. It was established in 1988, by a group of researchers and social activists. Their motive was to allocating and guiding the social endeavors and civil activities. It is meant to follow-up the domestic regional and international affairs, by means of researches, studies and data-collection.

The center has undergone two stages

1. The formative stage which witnessed the setting of the research materials and preparation of the fundamental structure.

2. The productive stage during which the Center was equipped by a strict scientific system for performance control, with an optimum utilization of modern technologies whether in receiving or sending data.

The center relies in its publications on a dedicated team of researchers, specialists in documentation, and experts in programming, besides a group of academicians and intellectuals.

The entire publications of the center are supervised and authorized by a scientific committee.

The means
The center seeks to accomplish these mentioned objectives through the following

1. Preparing reports, studies consultations in areas of

concern to the center

2. Doing field surveys and statistical studies

3. Building a data-bank and press archive

4. Publishing scientific and documentary periodicals and books

5. Organizing conferences workshops and panels

6. Accomplishing the data programs.

The Center as well has a toll of achievements:

1. Preparing more than 300 studies and reports in various fields.

2. Accomplishing a whole development field survey which covered a vast area of the Lebanese territories (1990-1992).

3. Accomplishing a survey of the political and electoral trends which included 400,000 voters the night before the parliamentary elections in 1996.

4. Assisting governmental departments ministries and international institutes in accomplishing several field projects.

5. Proceeding in analysis a number of numerous projects such as Alisar

6. The highway's network

. Conducting several specialized panels discussion about substantial issues7

Setting up a journal archive consisting (till the end of Dec20) of 500.000 essays i.e. approximately 2000.000 sheet selected from 150 local Arabic and international periodicals saved on microfilm

8. Documenting and analyzing the contents of the official Lebanese issue since 1980

9. Documenting the entire resistance operations against the Israeli occupation and the Israeli aggressions since 1982.

10. Linking the frames of databank users to the main server through outside computer stations

11. Founding a specialized library which includes 15000 volumes books, reports, and about 500 maps.

Exemplary Slogan

The preceding has been an exploration of the *Party of God* Documentation Center. Although it shows a promising benefit to culture and education however, a look at their media work would bring out the messages that are included in mourning rituals. These slogans were portrayed in the streets of the city Nabatieh, South Lebanon to commemorate "Karbala 'a" where the ancestors of Prophet Mohammad (people of the House) were murdered. Karbala 'a is a city in Iraq, where the battle (Ten Days) took place this is why the naming of the battle was taken after the timing as well, *Ashoura 'a* meaning ten days.

Putnam & Fairhurst (2001) state, "language is more than elements of narrative structure and words that reflect themes, rules, and norms of behavior" (p. 78). Indeed it is for within it there are various cultural codes and significations. The authors go on to state, "Structural variables such as occupation, subculture groups, and hierarchical position also contribute to variations in linguistic repertories. Specifically, scientists, especially biochemists, rely on technical and empirical talk in professional discourse but switch to contingency language in informal interactions about the field" (p. 82).

For instance, women of *Hezbollah*, who are committed members in the organization call upon each other as "sisters". Another example, whenever, a prophet's or an Imam's name is mentioned the sentence "God's prayers be upon him", or "peace upon him" will follow. The slogans say:

Everyday is Ashoura 'a (refers to tenth day battle, because the days of the battle were ten) every land is Karbala 'a.

The slogan which is written in white ink on black cloth. Such design is suitable to the sad memory-obituary. The content of the slogan indicates that although the incident is celebrated once per year, however the people feel that it is continuous, through time and regardless of the land.

-*Peace be upon the lady foreigner, the not at fault, the hostage, Zeinb the beautiful maiden.*

Zeinb is the daughter of the prophet Mohammed and she was taken as a captive in the battle and tortured, while she was watching her kinship murdered and tortured infront of her eyes. Such slogan is a reminder of the continuous propagation of the tragedy. In intercultural communication "Ashoura 'a," serves as being a narrative, a ritual that as well developed along the history of the *"Shia 'a"* sect in Islam.

-*Our case will not die at heart, when all hearts die.*

This saying is said by Imam Alrada [peace upon him]. Such slogans as well hold sayings of Imams as a reason to constant reminiscent of the Prophet's kinship.

-*Mouharam is that month were righteousness stands up and faces erroneous* Mouharam is a month in the Islamic Calendar, that month marks the death of the prophet's ancestors.

-*The loyal city dresses in woe and grief.*

Another reminder that the city is loyal and it shows its loyalty through various rituals of grievances that are customized through the sharp color black.

-*The love of Hussien is the method for achieving happiness, and his light has shed all through the place.*

It is an explanation that Imam Hussein, although was a martyr but the road he chose is surely the road for peace, and supplement.

-*A cry over the Hussein is a scream in the face of tyrannies.*

Don't be scared to shed tears over the beloved leader

Hussein, especially in a patriarchal society were men are accused of weakness when expressing sadness through tears. This cry, this expression of grief is only a manifestation of the oppression he, and the nation of *"Shia'a"* were subjected to.

-Oh- Hussien

A cry for Imam Hussein. In Arabic it is said "Wa husseinah", "wa" is a letter of emotional reference.

-If the tyrannies locked the doors of freedom, the youthful hands would open it.

This is a slogan emphasizing on the will power of manhood in defeating all types of oppression.

-You will always stay our dear icon in all generations to come- ye son of the prophet.

Continuous emphasis in following the road of the People of the house, and an everlasting mark they leave in the choices people make along their ways.

-Let the believer be righteous in meeting his lord.

The striking influence in this slogan is very much associated or directed towards men. In other words, be afraid not in meeting your God.

-Your love, the father of Abdullah, has taught us perseverance, and your martyrdom has lit our path.

Another exemplar of persistence in the right direction because the People of the House, and the battle of Ashoura'a has set a clear archetype of sacrifice.

-God have mercy over these hearts that burned for our sake.

A reminder of what type of sacrifice has been done for the sake of the *"Shia'a"* nation. These slogans as well can work as an explanation to Jihad and martyrdom that is practiced by the *Party of God.*

-I don't care when I die as a Muslim to what side I was stabbed.

An emphasis on the power of Islam in bringing out courage and diminishing all types of fear. A person would not care how he/she would die as long as they are Muslims.

-A nation that carries Hussein in its mentality will never die
An emphasis on the memory of the tragedy in bring forth subsistence to the nationhood.

-Ashoura'a [Battle of the ten days] is the battle where blood triumphed over the sword.
Another reminder that martyrdom is an everlasting victory

-I am the martyr of exemplars, every believer when remembering me would learn a lesson.
Hussein (P.) played an important factor in Shia'a Jihad. He is the martyr who was not afraid to face death, even if he was the only soldier in the battle. The slogan stresses on the lessons learned from the sacrifice of Hussein.

-The people of the house story in your generation is similar to Noah's Arc, whoever rides it is saved, and whomever did not drowned.
A metaphor is used here to make the story of the people of the house relative to Prophet Noah. The following argument will introduce the readers to more media productions planned by *Hezbollah*.

VIDEO-CD Productions

The structure of language away from its codes is of a vital importance as well. For instance the DVD that is titled *Jerusalem's Day*, in it, the *Party of God* are commemorating Jerusalem (Alkouds in Arabic), and at the same time they are parading and showing their military status. In the construction of the event, one could evidently notice the organized military structure. The military clusters were presented according to performance and function, and with consideration to age group, for instance, the young adults, are followed by the elderly (senior citizens) who as well formed a military group, and then followed by the children, later by women, one would clearly notice [and read] an evident show of power, organization, performance, unifications, and their constructions, even in speech presentations, word constructions, and flag appearances: for instance, in Jerusalem Day, the march starts with a portrayal of magnified photos; One of Lebanon, others of leaders, displays of flags, Lebanon, Palestine, and the Islamic Resistance flag in such progression.

The organization and presentation of war, is not only a power show, but also a power show to how well equip the *Party of God* is for that day. And although there were speeches made at that day, mainly to show respect, and to identify the factions within the military, the photos of the events form a visual code. The portrayal of photos of the air force weapons that they have, and the various small talks among the society within *Hezbollah* and surrounding it, about the small "toy like" plane that was able to break through Israeli land reinforce the power of Jihad. Such images are words dedicated to the inner and outside society. The presence of well-known leaders at that time, such as *Nasrallah*, and presence of the previous military defense minister, Abed al-Raheem Mourad emphasized the importance of the event. The prayers over the souls of the martyrs was a reminder for those who are in the show of their destiny, and a reminder to the audience that there are still people who are not scared of death. Kids, the code of continuation, displayed an acrobatic theme, to speak of their preparation to take over the mission at some point of time. But one of the most echoing performances of language presented in the DVD was the scream of the crowds saying: "Jerusalem, *Hezbollah* are coming".

When the *Party of God* speaks out, there has to always be a certain type of religious or political event at play. One of the latest events where *Nasrallah* spoke was that when he called for a pro Syria demonstration in the "Martyrs' Square" in Beirut in the spring of 2005. *Nasrallah* used a "directive" act of speech. Putnam & Fairhurst (2001) state that "directives are speech acts that convey requests, invitations, instructions, orders, and/or command directives use words that soften the impact of requests and avoid triggering offense, such as might, could, okay, and right" (p. 90). When calling for the demonstration *Nasrallah* used a shocking language, what I mean by shocking is that he used the formal and the informal speech. He formally called for the demonstration "we invite on next Tuesday at three o'clock p.m. to a wide crowd demonstration that is peaceful in Ryiad al-Soleh square next to the ESQUA building", then *Nasrallah* follows the invitation with a mockery criticism of the press saying "you could widen the zoom of your camera, or narrow it". Such statement is to previously pinpoint the role of the mass media in circumference and size the event.

Power is the primary construction in the speech of *Nasrallah*, especially when it comes to threats of battles. In the same event he asks the crowds "You Lebanese people, are you afraid of the United States forces?" the crowd answers loudly "No". He continues in a past, present and future line of thought "These forces came here previously, and if it comes in again it shall be defeated". The collective power, force and unification is in climax when he says "we empathize with martyr-president Rafek Al-Harri family, they gave blood sacrifice, and we know what it is like to give blood sacrifices, we stood against tyranny and defeated it, but today, as unified Lebanese crowd, unified with our will, military, resistance, we are stronger then any past time, and as for the Israeli 's, our friends, the Palestinians, will defeat you with their strong fists, and what you were not able to attain through war, I swear by God, that you will not have through politics". Such speech holds so much of framing. Putnam & Fairhurst (2001) state that "framing, as the fourth area of cognitive linguistic studies, refers to worldviews, fields of vision, or perspective for managing meaning" (p. 88). And the meaning here is double edged, although the rhetoric of *Nasrallah* states that the *Party of God* will not give up Palestine, however there is a declaration that the Palestinians shall be on the front line.

"By simply being uttered, words such as promising, requesting, warning, asserting, and apologizing performs through what is said" (Putnam & Fairhurst 2001, p. 90). *Nasrallah* uses metonymy in his speech when he says: "Syria shall stay the house of pride of the lion". Putnam & Fairhurst (2001) state that "Metonymy is a figure of speech in which the whole stands for *Hezbollah*, for example the use of the word heart to stand for emotions" (p. 108). In here, *Nasrallah* used it by presenting the Syrian President Alasad, which means lion, as a place to signify the respect to the king of the jungle, the strong and powerful, president and country-Syria, which by the way means in Aramic: the sun. Meanwhile, "a synecdoche, reverses this process by using the part to signify the whole, for example the term crown or throne to represent the king or the queen" *Nasrallah* used such terminology ornament when he represents the country or the enemy by the character of the prime minister "a word for Israel, Shalloum, Moufaz, and Sharon, cut off your hopes and put off your dreams of having Lebanon, you have no place in Lebanon". Slogans, jargon, clichés, and credos also function as synecdoche to represent an organization 's image. For instance, the logo of the Al-manar television station which is written in Arabic old font, using the color yellow, which coincides with the meaning of the word *Al-Manar*, the lighthouse, and the color yellow which is associated with *Hezbollah* as a whole. Some of these clichés are sad and that is always a set of frame work. There is always a cry, for instance in one of the tapes that is titled, "How Islam envisions Life", *Nasrallah* image is in his formal, usual dress, with his hand on his face, covering his eyes. A title supposedly to speak of the vision of Islam on life, *Nasrallah* has his eyes closed, maybe he is looking for an internal reflection, but he looks pretty sad. Is that how Islam envisions life, sadness! Many verses of the *Quran* proves the opposite, that Islam calls to enjoy life, that is a gift from God, even *Nasrallah* calls for it in the tape, but its seems that the metaanalysis or the group of media executives working with the *Party of God* has a certain vision in mind that it needs to portray. Among that sadness, misery of battles and war and whether surveyed, or not in the future, people in Lebanon, at some point have had it with war and its consequences, and they sure do need a "happy" peaceful break.

Chapter VI
Towards a Better Understanding of *Hezbollah*, *Shia'a*, Islam, and Cultural Rhetoric

Communication in the Arab World is particular in theory and application, and it is quite the same for *Hezbollah* due to the specificity of the context. Many cultures, organizations or/and movements are particular in case. When considering the Arab world and the Islamic nation in general it has to be taken in consideration that the nation is not completely solid, rather a flux of changes and transformations. Because changes are occurring, they are, indeed, gradual. Moving from a pre-modern society into a modernized one especially in Lebanon, envelops communication within the Arab world with such specialty that does not allow a complete, total and sudden import of the Western ideology. Although the American and the Arabic/Islamic cultures are in a state of tension now, we have to keep in mind that the tension constitutes the surface of the relationship, and within such tension there are bridges of intercultural exchange. While there is the reality of conflict, there is also the possibility of mediation.

The Arab world is strategically located holding a significant portion of civilization's meanings. It is at some point the focus of the world, and *Hezbollah* is part of that focus. To understand Islam, Shiaism and *Hezbollah*, this dissertation has served at answering the following questions through five chapters.

In Chapter I, I presented an overview of *Hezbollah*, my critical methodology and methods of data collection. Chapter I provided the rationale for this study, which centered on better understanding the rhetorical nature of *Hezbollah* as a social movement.

In chapter II, I found out that the rhetorical origin of the party of God is ultimately rooted in an Arabic rhetorical tradition that reflects narrative and Islamic values. *Hezbollah* in particular is influenced by Iranian and Lebanese, historical traditions, and even modern and postmodern thinking. Such findings were supplemented by narratives coming from *Hezbollah's* own rhetorical presentation. Context as well played in the formation of the *Party of God*. If it weren't for war, marginalization, and *Shia'a* weakness during the 1980s, the party would not have found a receptive audience. Hence, there was a need for such movement. And with *Hezbollah's* name (God's promised victory), the Shia'a were able to create power out of weakness.

The *Party of God* mediates and accommodates diverse constructions of ethnicity, race and color through its organizational structure. Since the movement is associated with Islam, it calls for equity among people, and these teachings are the direct rules of conduct.

Chapter III demonstrated these manifestations rhetorically both within *Hezbollah* and Islam. The issue of feminism was discussed as an element within the movement, and stories from the *"Series of the Resistant Women"* were discussed. Issues of dress codes, conduct, pleasure marriage, etc. were as well discussed as subjects of diverse construction within that organization. In sum, *Hezbollah* could be considered to be a premature diverse movement and a transformative movement, this interpretation may not be apparent to the outsider. The *Party of God* also has a potential to communicate with others, however, through varied channels of communication that range from public speeches to books and DVDs.

Nasrallah is the present acting General Secretary of the *Party of God*. In chapter II, the symbolic construction of leadership was explored. Leadership rhetoric was focused on the present leader, *Nasrallah*, and his leading policy and social significance. It was presented through a historical perspective on *Hezbollah* and consecutive leaders within its short history. It was argued too through a historical look at leadership conceptualization within Islam, and Shia'aism. The chapter also included narratives of Western construction to make the cultural and organizational behavior of the *Party of God* clearer. These narratives were taken from stories of "One Thousand and One Nights" and Western anthropological significations.

In Chapter IV, I examined rhetorical artifacts of the *Party of God*. Slogans, and brochures were described, interpreted and evaluated.

Moving from a diverse banquet of material and narratives in Chapter IV, in Chapter V, I was able to describe the organizational reality of *Hezbollah* through these texts. One of the evident findings is that the *Party of God* advances Jihad as a primary strategy for creating unity and motivation among audiences.

These were the chapters' findings and summaries however, gathering the pieces would not equal the sum of its parts. *Hezbollah* is not an isolated movement. It is acting and reacting, adapting to changes in the social context through a variable set of cultural performances.

Thus there is a need for communication inquiry that merges the contexts, projects an Arabic entity which converses with the relative Western and Eastern world. Communication channels like this, and similar scholarly work, would allow an understanding that can converse with diverse tongues historically and presently, and can develop special critiques of representation, demonstration, and above all communication. Aspects of the Arab rhetorical tradition here emerged onto the world's awareness with urgency and suddenness. My critique of *Hezbollah* provides an alternative frame for understanding ongoing resistance and reformation that will surely continue to capture the world's attention.

God in the Quran did not say that the Jewish are close to me, nor the Christians or the Muslims or Sunni or Shias or Buddhism. God says in the Quran that those who are proclaimed by my generosity are those who respect me most. Thus to be God's Party requires an adhesive manner of respect.

Reference

Assadallahy, M. (2004). *Islamists in a diverse society: Hezbollah in Lebanon as a case study*. Lebanon, Beirut. Arab Scientific Publishers.

Akbar, A. (1992*). Postmodernism and Islam: Predicament and Promise*. Routledge: London.

Alexander, B. K. (1999). Performing culture in the classroom: An instructional (auto) ethnography. *Text and Performance Quarterly*, *19*, 307-331.

Agar, M. (1986). *Speaking of ethnography*. Beverly Hills: Sage Publications.

Al-Jabouri, Y. (2002). *The Concept of God. Qum*. Iran: Ansariyan Publications.

Allahyari, H. (2003). *The Book of Occultation*. Qum. Iran: Ansariyan Publications.

Ball, P. (2004). *Critical mass: How one thing leads to another*. Arrow Books. The Random House Group Limited.

Bazi, M. (2004). *This is how Nasrallah conversed*. Lebanon: Dar Alameer Publishing.

Belsey, C. (1994). *Critical Practice*. Routledge: British Library Cataloguing in Publication.

Bochner, A. P. (2002). *Perspectives on inquiry III: The moral*

133

of stories. In M.L. Knapp & J. A. Daly (Eds.), Handbook of interpersonal communication (3rd ed.) (pp. 73-101). Thousand Oaks: Sage.

Brown, R. (1995).(Ed.). *Postmodern representations: Truth, power, and mimesis in the human sciences and public culture.* Urbana: IL. University of Illinois Press.

Burgchardt, C.(Ed.). (1995). *Readings in rhetorical criticism.* State College, Penn: Strata Publishing Company.

Chagall, M. (1999). *Arabian Nights.* NY: Prestel Verlag: Pagasis Library.

Conquergood, D. (1983). Communication as performance: Dramaturgical dimensions of everyday life. In J. Sisco (Ed.). *The Jensen Lectures: Contemporary Communication Studies.* Tampa: University of South Florida.

El-Koussa, K. (2001). *Pythagoras-the Math-magician.* Lebanon: Dar-Alameer Publishing.

Dickens, D. & Fontana, A.(Ed.). (1994). *Postmodernism and social inquiry.* New York: The Guilford Press.

Fairhurst, G. (2001). Communication competence. In L.L. Putnam & F. M. Jablin (Eds.), The new handbook of organizational communication (pp. 78-136). Thousand Oaks, CA: Sage.

Garrett, M. (1999). Some elementary methodological reflections on the study of the Chinese rhetorical tradition. In A. Gonzalez & D. Tanno (Eds.). *Rhetoric in intercultural contexts* (pp. 53-63) Thousand Oaks, CA: Sage.

Garret, M. &Xiao, X. (1994). The rhetorical situation revisited. *Rhetoric and Society Quarterly, 23,* 30-40.

Geertz, C. (1973). *The interpretation of cultures.* New York: Basic Books.

Gharib, A. (2002). *Inside Hizbu'llah: Politics and religion.* London: Pluto Press.

Golden, J. Berquist, & G. Coleman, W. (1992). *The rhetoric of western thought* (5ᵗʰ Ed.). Kerper Boulevard, IA: Kendell/ Hunt Publishing Company.

Giddens, A. (1991). *Modernity and self identity.* Stanford, Calif.: Stanford University Press.

Glesne, C. (1999). *Becoming qualitative researchers: An introduction.* University of Vermont: Addison Wesley Longman.

Hamada, B. I. (2001). The Arab image in the minds of western image-makers. *The Journal of International Communication* (7-35).

Jablin F. M., L.L. & Sias, P. M. (2001). Communication Competence. In L.L. Putnam & F. M. Jablin (Eds.), *The new handbook of organizational communication* (pp. 78-136). Thousand Oaks, CA: Sage.

Jameson, F. (1997). *Postmodernism, or the cultural logic of late capitalism.* Duke University Press, Durham.

Kassem, N. (2005). *Hizbullah: The story from within.* Dalia Khalil (Trans.). London: West Bourne Grove.

Kraidy, M. (2004). Introduction. In P. Murphy & M. Kraidy (Eds.) *Global media studies: Ethnographic perspectives.* New York: Routledge.

Knapp, M.L., Daly, J.A., Albada, K.F., & Miller, G. R. (2002). Background and current trends in the study of interpersonal communication. In M. L. Knapp &J. A. Daly (Eds.) *Handbook of interpersonal c communication* (3rd ed.) (pp. 3-20). Thousand Oaks: Sage. Lull, J. (2000). *Media, communication, culture: A global approach.* New York: Columbia University Press.

Lindlof, R.T. (1995). *Qualitative communication research methods.* Thousand Oaks: Sage Publications.

Lyotard, J.F. (1992). *The postmodern explained.* translated by

Barry, D. Maher, B. Pefanis, J. Spate, V. and Thomas, M. Translation edited by Pefanis, J. and Thomas, M. Minnesota: University of Minnesota Press, Minneapolis.

Maxwell, J.A. (1996). *Qualitative research design: An interpretive approach.* Thousand Oaks: Sage.

Middleton, J. (1967). Myth and cosmos: Readings in mythology and symbolism.Garden City, New York: The American Museum of Natural History Press.

Murray, P. (2000). *Classical Literary Criticism-Penguin Book.* Penguin Group.

Nasr, S. (2004). *Shi'ah: Islamic Republic of Iran,* Qum: Ansariyan Publications

Philipsen, G. (1992). *Speaking culturally: Explorations in social communication.* State University of New York Press, Albany.

Reed, M. (1996). Organizational theorizing: A historically contested terrain. In S. R. Clegg, C. Hardy, & W. Nord (Eds.). *Handbook of organizational studies* (pp. 31-56). London: Sage.

Roberts, R. (1925). *The social laws of the Qur'an: Considered and compared with those of the Hebrew and other ancient codes.* London: Williams and Norgate, LTD.

Schechner, R. (1988). *Performance theory.* New York and London. Routledge.

Streek, J. (2002). Culture, meaning, and interpersonal communication. In M.L. Knapp & J. A. Daly (Eds.). *Handbook of interpersonal communication* (3rd ed.) (pp. 73-101). Thousand Oaks: Sage.

Tracy, K. (2002). *Everday talk: Building and reflecting identities.* NY: The Guilford Press.

Endnotes:

[1] *Hezbollah*: meaning the party of God. Throughout the research it is going to be italized. Other times it will appear without emphasis when it is cited and the readers are familiar with the concepts. There are various pronunciations of the word and accordingly the spelling might vary.

[2] Abdullah: The name is a hybrid of: *Abed* which means worshipper. *Allah*, means God.

[3] Through out the study, readers will notice that the word Prophet Mohammad is followed by (PBUH) the abbreviation of the sentence Peace be upon him. Or simply (p) for the same prayer. In Muslim society it is considered a blessing to always follow the name of the Prophet or Imam with a prayer. In the study, I sometimes follow the Islamic rule, and in others I would keep the prayer in the heart to allow the flow of the argument.

[4] PLO: In Arabic it is *Munazzamat al-Tahrir al-Filastiniyyah*, a political and paramilitary organization of Palestinians dedicated to the establishment of an independent Palestinian state in the region historically known as Palestine

Printed in the United Kingdom
by Lightning Source UK Ltd.
119035UK00001B/9

Does God Have a Party?

Rhetorical Examination of Hezbollah

By Dr. Souhad Kahil

PublishAmerica
Baltimore

First printing

At the specific preference of the author, PublishAmerica allowed this work to remain exactly as the author intended, verbatim, without editorial input.

ISBN: 1-4241-6308-0
PUBLISHED BY PUBLISHAMERICA, LLLP
www.publishamerica.com
Baltimore

Printed in the United States of America